MADE TO BE ME

MADE TO BE ME

A powerful story of faith, hope and transformation

Shell Perris

Authentic

MILTON KEYNES ● COLORADO SPRINGS ● HYDERABAD

14 13 12 11 10 09   8 7 6 5 4 3 2 1

First published 2009 by Authentic Media
9 Holdom Avenue, Bletchley, Milton Keynes, MK1 1QR, UK
1820 Jet Stream Drive, Colorado Springs, CO 80921, USA
Medchal Road, Jeedimetla Village, Secunderabad 500 055, A.P., India
www.authenticmedia.co.uk

Authentic Media is a division of IBS-STL UK, limited by guarantee, with its
Registered Office at Kingstown Broadway, Carlisle, Cumbria, CA3 0HA.
Registered in England & Wales No. 1216232. Registered
charity 270162

British Library Cataloguing in Publication Data

A catalogue record for this book is available from the British Library
ISBN: 978-1-86024-760-6

Cover Design by fourninezerodesign.
Print Management by Adare
Printed in Great Britain by J. F. Print, Sparkford

CONTENTS

Contents

INTRODUCTION

Have I lived an ordinary life? Yes, I suppose I have. Did I have a good upbringing? Yes, I guess I did. Am I happy with my life? Yes, extremely happy. So, I hear you ask, why am I writing this book?

I have written this book to bring hope to the hopeless; to show that ordinary people living ordinary lives still face trials and times of testing. I have written this book as an attempt to illustrate the fact that the choices we make can affect our whole lives. I believe with all of my heart that God directs our footsteps but we choose our paths. Ultimately, I have written this book to prove that we can overcome and recover from what was and learn to live in freedom and victory once again.

The truth is, whether we like it or not, we all have a past and we all have locked doors that if opened would reveal things about us we would never want others to know about or see. The vast majority of us live with memories of sadness, or of hurt, or even of regret. We all know what it's like to lose a loved one. We all know what it's like to seek approval. Many of us know what it's like to be bullied and that growing up can be a difficult task!

In writing this book I have chosen to unlock a few of those doors and let you, the reader, into the little corners of my life. But those little corners have made me who I am today. Without them I would not be doing what I am doing, I wouldn't have the characteristics I have and I wouldn't live the way I now live.

I am not ashamed to unlock those doors and invite you into what was my world and what is now my world. I just hope and pray that you won't stay the same once you have walked away from my world and back into yours.

I am not telling you my story because I am looking for sympathy or pity. I realise that my experience of having an eating disorder is not the worst case in the world by any stretch of the imagination. Millions of people suffer from some sort of eating disorder across the world and many of them end up walking a lot further down the road than I did. I wasn't hospitalised or fed through tubes, I didn't take laxatives or eat tissue paper soaked in orange juice, but my experience of having anorexia nervosa was real for me.

I struggled for over three years with something that I started off in control of but which very quickly took control of me. I understand what it's like to feel worthless, unlovable, confused and lost, as many of us do. But I also know how it feels to fight through it and win.

Sometimes it takes an earth-shattering wake-up call for us to appreciate things and realise that life shouldn't be about just getting on with it and hoping all ends well. Life should be about living . . . and I mean really living;

making the most of opportunities; taking risks every now and then; understanding that being comfortable, going to university, having a nice house, a husband/wife and 2.4 children isn't necessarily the be all and end all of life! Having an eating disorder was like having an earth-shattering wake-up call. Do you know what? I have reached a point now where I am so grateful to God for allowing me to go through that time.

Another reason for writing this book is to show you that there is a light at the end of the tunnel even though it doesn't always feel that way. I want to encourage you in your current situations; to challenge you to dream for the future and to inspire you to be the person that you ultimately want to be and, more importantly, the person that God desires you to be. I have learnt the hard way in many ways, but please believe me when I say this: living life without God is nothing compared to living life with God. Before I had an eating disorder I was quite satisfied with my life . . . or so I thought. It wasn't perfect and the question I asked more than any other question was 'What if?' But despite that, I was generally content. However, after having an eating disorder and finding God in the midst of that, I realised that there was so much more to life.

This book is split into two sections for a reason. 'The Old Me' is my life before I found God. 'The New Me' is my life since I have found God. I believe with all of my heart that God has the ability to transform lives. I also believe that we are all on a journey and we are all at very different stages. Some of you will be totally closed about the whole 'God thing' to the point where you shut this book now and never pick it up again. Some of you will be a little more open-minded and may not have found God for yourselves but are interested in wanting to know a little bit more. Some of you will read the pages of this book and relate to every word that is said because you have already found God and you know about the difference he can make in our lives. Many of you will begin to read this book thinking you know God and finish reading this book wanting to know God so much more!

Wherever you're at and whatever situations you're facing at this moment in your life please know this: God has the ability to transform your life just like he has transformed mine . . . and when I use the word 'transform' I don't mean transformation in the way we know it – I mean unimaginable, life-changing, revolutionary transformation! The question is . . . are you ready for it?

I will finish this introduction in the same way that I started it. Have I lived an ordinary life? Yes, I suppose I have. Did I have a good upbringing? Yes, I guess I did. Am I happy with my life? Yes, extremely happy. So, I hear you ask, why am I writing this book?

I may be an ordinary girl but I serve an extraordinary God and, because of that and the way he has transformed me, I have the privilege of leading an extraordinary life. All the glory well and truly belongs to God.

THE OLD ME

CHAPTER 1

A LITTLE BIT ABOUT ME

On 29 September 1984 at 3.03 p.m. Michelle Leanne Whittaker (that's me!) entered the world weighing 7lb 6oz.

I spent most of my childhood living on the outskirts of Warrington in north-west England with my mum, dad and younger brother, Craig. We had a dog called Leasha, followed by a dog called Shanti and another dog called Asha. Along the way we've also had a rabbit called Thumper, a hamster called Tammy (who we thought was a boy but turned out to be a girl!), a fish tank full of random tropical fish, and five budgies called Bobby 1, Bobby 2, Robbie, Georgie, and Andy. We didn't have all of these pets at one time of course, but the 'Whittaker Zoo' was always kept well stocked! And, just in case you're wondering, the reason for having so many budgies was because for some bizarre and unknown reason, I didn't have a very good technique when it came to keeping them alive! Bobby 1 died, then Bobby 2 died, then Robbie (who I'd named after Robbie Williams when he was in Take That) died and so on and so on until I couldn't stand the pain of losing any more budgies. Actually, that is a slight exaggeration. When my mum told me that Andy had died, I responded by saying, 'Oh well, never mind. I don't think I want another one because they don't seem to last very long, do they?'

My mum, Valerie, worked in a bank as I was growing up and now works as a personal assistant at a college in Warrington. My dad is a policeman and my brother is an actor. Mum and Dad met each other at high school (the same high school that my brother and I went to) whilst performing in a school musical together and got married when they were pretty young . . . Mum was 18 and Dad was 20. I am really proud to say that after twenty-six years of marriage my parents are still happy and tog-ether. It just goes to show that young love can last . . . with a lot of hard work and commitment of course!

As a little girl I didn't really follow a stereotypical 'girly-girly' path. I hated playing with Barbie dolls and plastic babies (give me an Action Man any day!), I was not at all interested in other people doing my hair for me, and I was scarily independent . . . in fact, I would go as far as saying that I was a complete and utter brat at times! I knew exactly what I wanted and if I didn't get it I would scream and scream until everyone knew about it! Thank goodness I'm not like that any more! (Although I'm pretty sure that if you asked my hubby about that he'd quite possibly disagree!) My mum used to read me a nursery rhyme about a 'little girl who had a little curl, right in the middle of her forehead'. It went on to say that 'when she was good she was very very good but when she was bad she was horrid!' I still believe to this day that it was written about me!

I remember reaching a stage in my early life, when I was about 5 years old, and the only thing I wanted was to be like Kylie Minogue. I wanted to sing like Kylie, dance like Kylie and look like Kylie. So I thought I'd start off by singing down a hairbrush in front of my mirror in my bed-room, pretending to be a pop star. Whenever my mum and dad had friends or family round I'd always end up standing in the middle of the lounge and swishing my skirt from side to side as I attempted to sing a Cliff Richard song at the top of my voice. 'Cliff Richard?' I hear you ask. Yes – I'm afraid and very ashamed to say that I used to sing Cliff Richard songs. Don't blame me – blame my mother. She's the one with the obsession!

The next step in trying to achieve my ambition of being like Kylie was dance lessons. So I started going to a modern dance class that was held in a local church hall on a Monday evening. After the modern dance class there was a tap dancing class, so I joined that too! Then I was told that there were ballet classes on a Saturday morning in the same church hall and so I found myself attending all three classes on a weekly basis.

Finally, it came to the most essential yet the most challenging part . . . looking like Kylie! I'll never forget one particular event that happened in a well-known clothes shop in Warrington town centre. I found a gorgeous dress that looked exactly like something Kylie would wear, and I fell in love with it straight away. I had a very clear idea of what I wanted and this dress was it.

I ran over to my mum, grabbed her hand and dragged her over to the rail where the sacred dress was hanging. I looked at it in awe, and then looked up to my mum and said, 'What do you think?'

My mum took one look at it and replied, 'You're not wearing that!'

Boy, did I scream! 'I want that dress! I want that dress! Why won't you let me have that dress?' I started kicking my legs, crying out loud and having the biggest temper tantrum ever right in the middle of the shop.

However, my mum wasn't having any of it. She simply dragged me out of the shop and I never saw the dress again. I think my mum had this idea that I was going to get a pretty, girly dress with flowers on it but I was determined to get a dress like Kylie. In the end we compromised and chose a dress together that was black velvet at the top with a royal blue and black polka-dot rah-rah skirt attached. Sounds lovely doesn't it?! Let me tell you though, it was highly fashionable at the time!

My problem was this – when I was 5 I wanted to be 15, when I was 15 I wanted to be 25 and now that I've reached my mid-twenties I just want to stay at this age forever because I don't want to get any older than I am now. I want to be like Peter Pan and live in Never-Never Land. Oh well . . . at least I can dream!

Now we get on to the subject of school. I went to a Church of England primary school called St Thomas's. I don't think it was because my mum and dad were particularly 'religious' or anything. I just went there because it was a good school.

We very rarely went to church when I was growing up. I was christened as a baby and confirmed when I was 12 but I wouldn't say we were 'regular churchgoers'. For me church was the most boring thing on the planet. I never quite saw the sense in going to an old-fashioned building to sit on a wooden, highly uncomfortable, communal bench for an hour and a half and then be made to listen to someone talk on and on about stuff that was totally irrelevant to me. And to top it all off, it was like making any noise whatsoever was seen to be of the devil, and so for the whole hour and a half my parents said nothing to me but 'sssssshhh'!

However, the worst bit (by far) was having to wear your 'Sunday best' clothes. Apparently God didn't 'approve' if I were to wear jeans or t-shirts in church. Oh no – it had to be fancy blouses, smart trousers or skirts, polished shoes and pristine hairstyles. Have you ever heard so much rubbish in your life?! You can imagine why I wasn't jumping for joy when I found out I had to get up and go to church on a Sunday morning. Staying in bed and watching weekend television was far more appealing. In fact, anything was more appealing than going to church.

I don't think I ever had a personal faith as a child. I remember being told that you could talk to God by praying but the only prayers I prayed were ones that would make my life a bit better – 'Dear God, please make my mum and dad buy me a new computer game . . . please tell my brother to stop bugging me . . . please let school be cancelled in the morning.' The funniest thing was that I thought the prayers would only be answered if I looked out of my bedroom window and stared at the moon as I was saying them. I even thought that the longer I looked at the moon the more likely that whatever I was praying for was going to happen. Believe me, I spent hours looking at that flippin' moon. No wonder my prayers were never answered!

I remember my very first day at primary school so well. I had been playing on my slide in the garden during the summer and, as a result of getting a little too excited, I had ended up running into an open window and cutting my head open. I had to go to hospital to have several stitches. I even got a special certificate for being such a brave girl! I introduced myself to the other children in my class by saying, 'Hello! My name is Michelle and my head is sewn together with blue and red thread. Do you wanna see?' It was a great story to begin my school life with!

St Thomas's was a lovely little school with seven year groups. Each year group had one class that consisted of approximately thirty children. Everyone wanted to go to St Thomas's because, when I was there, it wasn't compulsory to wear the uniform. There was an optional uniform (a royal blue sweatshirt, grey skirt/trousers and a white shirt or polo shirt) but if you didn't want to wear it you could just turn up in your own clothes. However, for some totally unfair and unjust reason, my mum insisted that I had to wear the school uniform Monday through to Thursday. I was only allowed to wear my own clothes on a Friday – if I had behaved well that week. I absolutely hated it and the worst bit was that I was one of the few people in the whole school who were made to wear school uniform. The vast majority of my class wore their own clothes every day and they used to make fun of me because I had to wear school uniform. That was my first experience of being bullied.

I was brought up to believe that you could do anything if you put your mind to it. I used to try so hard in school and realised quite quickly that my mum was right – you could do anything if you put your mind to it. I was the sort of child that would keep trying and trying until I got it right. I never gave up and I never settled for second best. If I was going to do something, whether it be school work or something creative, I was going to do it well. I suppose this came from another of my mum's little life mottos, 'If it's worth doing, it's worth doing well' and 'If at first you don't succeed, try and try again.'

However, I also realised that doing things well and achieving good grades was not something that other people thought acceptable . . . in fact quite the opposite. Other people, at times, found it threatening and 'un-cool' and would typecast me as a 'swot' or a 'teacher's pet'. By the time I was in Year 4 I was very aware that I didn't 'cut it' when it came to popularity contests. I didn't really have many friends and I was becoming more and more aware of the social and moral divides within my class. If I wanted to do well in school and keep my head down I was going to have to sacrifice the approval of many of my classmates and get ready for the bumpy ride ahead.

I was not a naughty child at school and I hated the thought of being told off, especially by adults other than my mum and dad. I'll always remember the time I got told off by my Year 4 teacher, Mrs Kingdon, when I was 9 years old.

There were about ten of us sat round a table doing our work. The side door was open and it was a beautiful, sunny day. We were daring each other to throw a pen lid out of the door and run out to get it without Mrs Kingdon noticing!

After a while we got bored and decided to start a conversation about my friend's mum. My friend was saying that her mum had said that sex was the best thing ever. We were at the age where we didn't really know what sex was but thought that it was rude and something to giggle uncontrollably about.

She then went on to talk about lesbians . . . and before you ask, I haven't got a clue how we got on to that particular topic of conversation! I was a very innocent and naïve child and didn't know anything about 'the birds and the bees' but I was also very inquisitive and didn't like not knowing what other people were talking about. So, at the top of my voice I interrupted the chitchat and said, 'What's a lesbian?'

The whole class went silent and Mrs Kingdon shouted, 'Michelle! Come here!'

I immediately went bright red, got out of my chair and sheepishly walked over to where Mrs Kingdon was sitting. 'What did you say?' she asked in a rather stern voice.

'What's a lesbian?' I replied. I remember looking at her horrified face and feeling incredibly embarrassed as I stood there with my head bowed down in shame.

'I think that's something you should ask your mum, Michelle,' she said. As I turned around to walk back to my chair she continued by shouting, 'And don't let me ever catch you saying that again!'

I got back to my seat and my friends all started sniggering but I was still overwhelmed by humiliation. For some reason I was always the one who got caught on the odd occasion that I did do something wrong!

So, as you're probably starting to work out, school was a place where I felt like I didn't really fit in. I wanted to do well and I was encouraged to do well but I desperately wanted to be accepted by my friends. I wanted them to laugh at my jokes and I wanted to be part of the 'in crowd'. I wanted to be invited to sleepovers and I wanted real friends that wanted to spend time with me. That's why wearing my own clothes was such a big deal for me. I thought that if I wore my own clothes every day, like everyone else, I would fit in with my friends and be more popular but that was never going to happen. In my eyes it was obvious that you couldn't have the best of both worlds.

When I was in the last year of primary school our class had a visit from one of the teachers from the nearby high school that the majority of us were going to be attending.

We were all given a form to fill in and we had to write down the names of two other people in our class who we wanted to be in a form with in high school. I wrote down the names of two of my friends . . . Kate and Amy. Then we all looked at each other's papers to see the names of the people we had written down. To my surprise and utter disappointment no one had written my name down. I was so upset and spent the next few months worrying about which of my so-called 'friends' I was going to be in a class with in high school.

We were eventually given a sheet with the class listings on. I remember searching frantically to see who I was in a class with. Luckily I was in a class with the two people I had written down but I still didn't like the fact that they didn't want to be in a class with me. That was how my high school journey began and it just seemed to get worse from there on in.

CHAPTER 2

STICKS AND STONES

I am not what
happened to me;
I am what I choose
to become.

In September 1996 I moved into Year 7 (first year) at Bridgewater High School in Warrington where there were now approximately three hundred students in each year group. It was a massive change for me and I suddenly felt like a little fish in a great big ocean. My life had dramatically changed overnight. All of a sudden I was in a huge school with hundreds of unfamiliar corridors. I had to make my own way to and from school and I was faced with responsibilities that I'd never had before.

At the same time it was an opportunity to start afresh and allow the real me to shine through . . . whoever the real me was. I had this idealistic dream that people would accept me for who I was and that I wouldn't get bullied any more. I dreamt that I would have lots of friends and a jam-packed social calendar, that being popular and working hard would go hand in hand.

I started high school with dreams but within a few months they had been entirely shattered.

I had some amazing teachers at school, one of which was my first-year form tutor, Mr Cuthbert. I was in a form group known as 7CB. In Year 7 we weren't split into ability groups or option groups. For every lesson of every day of every week all 30 of us were together as 7CB. In many ways it was great because we got to know each other really well. However, it also meant that if there was a problem you couldn't easily escape from it. Unfortunately, that was my experience of being in 7CB . . .

It started off quite well. Everyone seemed to be getting on with each other, there were no major character clashes and we were reasonably well behaved. As time went by we started to get to know who the naughty ones were, who the intelligent ones were, who the popular ones were, who the athletic ones were, who the loud ones were, etc. I didn't really fit into any category as such. I just worked hard, kept my head down and got on with things. I wasn't anti-social or arrogant with it but at the same time I wasn't the sort of person to attach myself to a group of friends and then never speak to anyone else. I chatted to anyone and everyone, respected classmates and teachers, smiled at people as I walked around the school, kept to the rules and generally tried to be a 'good' person.

Maybe that was my problem; maybe if I'd tried to stand out a bit more or had labelled myself as a certain type of person or even if I'd shown a bit of attitude once in a while I wouldn't have been bullied as much as I was. Was I 'too nice'? Was I 'too ordinary'? Was I 'too normal'? Did people not take to 'nice, ordinary, normal' people?

I was bullied constantly for three years. I felt like I had to fight every day for friendship. I was called horrible, nasty names. People wouldn't sit next to me in class. Even the people that I thought were my friends would talk about me behind my back and leave me out. And it wasn't just a few people . . . it was the majority.

I walked from lesson to lesson on my own. People used to make fun of me because I didn't roll my skirt up so that it was short like everyone else's. They'd bash into me in corridors and throw things at me. I'd walk past a classroom as people were lining up to go in and the whole class would start shouting things at me. As this happened to me more and more I could feel my inner self

being squashed and becoming less confident. I felt iso-
lated and unwanted. I felt like I couldn't trust anyone and
that feeling of loneliness was slowly taking over.

Lunchtimes were the worst – forty-five minutes with
nothing to do but sit on my own, eat lunch, and walk aim-
lessly round the school. One saving grace was that my
Auntie Lynda was a dinner lady at Bridgewater. When I'd
eaten my lunch I used to make my way over to her till and
just stand by her side as she served the other students.
On the days when she wasn't there I would sometimes
go into the music room and play the piano or sing a
song. No one saved me a seat or invited me to sit with
them. When I did sit with other people they would get up
and leave the table within five or ten minutes of me being
there and I would be left to finish off on my own. They
would leave their trays and plates and tell me to tidy their
mess up for them – and of course I did it because I was
afraid of being told off if I left them there.

I remember having days off every so often because it
would all get a bit too much for me. I would lie down on
the sofa with my head on my mum's knee just crying
because I was so fed up of being miserable at school. I
would have regular panic attacks because I was so
stressed about . . . well . . . everything. The thing is, when
you're at school it takes up a pretty big chunk of your life.
If you're the sort of person who really enjoys school then
it's great, but if you hate school it's not very good at all.

In the second year of high school I ended up moving
forms and found myself being a member of 8FX. I got in
with a really nice group of friends and even though I
never really trusted them, it was better than it had ever

been before. I still got called names, was shouted at, pushed around and left to do a lot of things on my own, but it was definitely an improvement.

Towards the end of my third year, things started to improve even more. The music/drama department had organised a theatre trip to go and see *Phantom of the Opera* at the Empire Theatre in Liverpool. Part of the trip-package was that a week or so later we were invited to go back to the Empire Theatre to do a master class with some of the cast members. It was a great opportunity and I remember being so excited.

As part of the master class, we had to prepare some creative sketches/songs that explored possible ideas for a *Phantom of the Opera* sequel. I went home and wrote two songs in one night – lyrics, melody, chords, the lot. I recorded them onto a cassette tape and took them into school the next day. I couldn't wait to play them to my music teacher, Miss Wolfenden, and when I did she was amazed. She asked me if I would perform them as part of the group performance in the master class and I did. I stood on the stage in the Empire Theatre and performed my songs to some of the cast members of *Phantom of the Opera*. I couldn't believe it!

When we got back to school I was asked to sing one of them in my year group assembly. I had never per-formed a song in school before and I remember being incredibly nervous – but I did it. I stood on stage in my Year 9 (third year) assembly and looked out at 300 faces. Not just any 300 faces: 300 faces of people who had caused me nothing but heartache and trauma for the last three years; 300 faces of people who had made my life a misery and who'd helped me to become lacking in con- fidence and insecure. In case you've not yet realised it, this was a big deal for me. I was shaking from head to toe as I stood there listening to the introduction, waiting to open my mouth and sing.

As I began to sing the assembly hall went silent . . . and for the next four minutes I sang my little heart out with every ounce of emotion and energy I had within me. As the song was coming to the end I began to wonder what people were going to think. Were they going to like it? Was it just going to be another thing that people would pick on me for doing? Was it going to be helpful or hindering?

The song finished, there was a brief pause and, to my astonishment, every set of hands in the assembly hall began to clap. I walked off the stage and people were still clapping. I sat in my seat and the people around me leaned towards me and said, 'Michelle, that was really good. Well done!' For the first time ever, my peers were commending me for what I'd just done. I walked around school that day with a spring in my step and a big fat smile on my face. 'Michelle Whittaker' had been labelled a 'good singer' and people, all of a sudden, started to take notice of me.

There were still people who didn't like me and I still had miserable days, but it was so much better than it used to be and any amount of improvement was good for me. I finished Year 9 with a glimmer of hope in my heart. Was Year 10 (fourth year) going to be a new beginning for me?

In many ways the answer was 'yes'. My school was split into two sites – years 7, 8 and 9 were on one site, and then down the road was the other site with years 10 and 11 and the sixth form.

It was a new school site, a new school year and I was doing new subjects. I had dropped geography, history, French, IT, food technology and CDT (all the subjects I didn't particularly enjoy) and I'd opted to do dance, drama, music, graphic design, RE, English language and literature, German, maths and double science. (I would like to add at this point that I hated maths and science but had to do them because they were compulsory. Sometimes I can't believe that I ended up marrying a science teacher! But hey, they do say opposites attract!) So school was indeed becoming a better place for me and I was beginning to develop a love for my life.

It would be my greatest pleasure to be able to stop writing now and pretend that my story ended there . . . that life was better than it ever had been and that it continued to get better and better forevermore – the end. But as you and I both know, life never seems to work out quite like that. There are always little challenges, mountains to climb, rivers to cross – hard times that are supposed to 'make us stronger'. If I could have a quid for every time someone has said to me, 'Oooh, cheer up love – there's always something better round the corner,' I'd be a millionaire by now! I don't know about you but every time I walk round one of 'life's little corners' there's always something there to try me . . . always something there to shove me well outside of my comfort zone and remind me that there's no such thing as an 'easy life'.

CHAPTER 3

MY MISSION

how you climb up the
mountain is just as important
as how you get down the
mountain. and so it is with life,
which for many of us becomes one
big gigantic test followed by one
big gigantic lesson. in the end, it
all comes down to one word...
GRACE.

So, by this time it was the beginning of September 1999. I was very nearly 15 years old and I'd just gone into Year 10 (fourth year) at high school. I'd had an amazing summer and had experienced my very first holiday romance with a lovely guy called Rob.

My mum and dad have owned a caravan since I was 8 years old, and in the summer of '99 my family and I went caravanning in the Lake District. Like most teenagers, I'd reached that funny stage where I wasn't a little girl any more but I wasn't an adult either. The question was this: should I ride around the campsite on my bike, shouting and screaming with all the other kids or should I do the more sophisticated thing of reading a book or a magazine whilst sunbathing by the lake? I remember seeing Rob, a tall, dark, handsome, older guy and thinking, *Sack the bike thing – I'm sunbathing!*

But of course I didn't sunbathe for the sake of sunbathing. Oh no – I was sunbathing to impress! The childish bathing suit was scrapped for the boob-enhancing bikini. The carefree 'come-as-you-are' holiday approach was replaced with the 'my hair and make-up has got to be perfect or else' approach. My mum or dad would walk into the caravan whilst I was grooming myself and ask the dreaded question, 'Who are you trying to impress?'

I would stutter and sweat and eventually say, 'No one,' whilst secretly thinking, *Rob . . . I'm trying to impress Rob!*

Well, you'll be pleased to know that all of my hard work paid off! A few nights into the holiday, Rob and I shared our first kiss whilst sitting beside the campfire. I remember going to bed that night and thinking to myself, *I am no longer a little girl – I'm a woman.* But then I decided that being a woman sounded too old so I'd just scrap the 'little' and say I was a girl instead!

Those two weeks were fantastic: walking hand in hand round the campsite, kissing around corners and trying not to get caught! Saying goodbye was heartbreaking. And then my heart was broken a little bit more when I got home and had a text from Rob saying that it was a great holiday fling but that's all it was. How rude! I melodramatically cried into my pillow for days. I sent him letters and text messages begging him to change his mind. But no, my holiday romance was going to stay a holiday romance. Oh well – how does that famous song go . . . 'Que sera sera, whatever will be will be'!

I then made the mistake of thinking that because I'd had a holiday fling with a guy who was three years older than me that I was grown up and could do whatever I fancied. My parents, on the other hand, had very different ideas . . . and so the battles commenced.

We argued constantly about where I was going, whether or not I was going, who I was going with, what time I had to be in for or what time I was going to get picked up. The phrases, 'You're not going out looking like that', 'If you're going to live under my roof you will live by my rules', 'What time do you call this?' and 'Right – you're grounded' were used quite regularly. Doors were slammed, walls were punched, tears were cried and floors were stamped on, but eventually apologies were made, hugs were given . . . and then the whole cycle would start all over again.

It sounds hilarious when you say it like that but I know for a fact that it wasn't at all funny at the time. I remember feeling like my whole world had collapsed on top of me. It was as if I didn't really live in a house – I lived inside a verbal boxing ring from the moment I woke up to the moment I went to bed and I'm pretty sure my parents felt that way too!

And so it was time to go back to school as a Year 10 'girl' (not a Year 9 'little girl') and work hard in my final two years of high school. I had quite a few friends at this point – not what I would call close friends and I certainly never had a best friend – but I was more content and my confidence was beginning to reappear.

My favourite subject was music, and I would spend most of my breaks and lunchtimes in the music room writing songs. I would sit at the piano and write about whatever I was feeling at the time. Most of the songs followed a teenage rebellious theme with titles such as, 'Be What You Want' and 'My Life'! You see I honestly felt that I had no control over my own life. My parents were finding it really difficult (just like every other parent out there) to 'let go' and I felt squashed and over-protected. My grandad had died when I was 12 years old, which was the first time I had ever experienced the loss of someone close to me. I remember feeling helpless and angry at the fact that I couldn't do anything about it. He had been taken away from me and that was it . . . gone in the blink of an eye. My mum went through a time of struggling with depression, my extended family was a 'bit messy', then my nana died very suddenly, and the memories of being bullied were still haunting me.

All of these things were happening around me and deeply affecting me, and all the time I was becoming more and more desperate for a sense of control. I suppose in many ways I wanted an idealistic life, one where I could say what did and didn't happen, one where I made my own decisions and had a say. It was like there was a little voice within me that was screaming at the top of its lungs but no one was hearing it. It was as if no one and nothing was taking any notice of what I wanted and how I felt. What about my opinions and my ways of doing things? What about what I thought? Did it not matter? Was I not allowed to be in control of anything in my life?

I didn't realise it at the time but I was on a mission . . . a mission to gain control. But it had to be a secret mission – something that no one else could know about. After all, it felt to me like being in control was forbidden. And so I made the decision to control the amount of food I ate. No one could make me eat if I didn't want to. No one could control how much food passed through my mouth. I wasn't a baby that relied on being spoon fed by other people. I was a 'girl' who was quite capable of feeding herself, or indeed not feeding herself. My mission began by choosing the easiest meal to skip . . . lunch.

My mum always gave me a packed lunch to take to school with me; home-made sandwiches, a piece of fruit, something sweeter like chocolate or a yoghurt, or a packet of crisps and a drink. Every morning I would walk from the bus stop, through the playground, into the school and the first thing I saw as I entered the school building was a big, green bin that resembled a large-scale fizzy drink can. I would check no one was looking, put the plastic bag that contained my lunch in the bin and walk off down the corridor to wherever I needed to be.

And do you know what the best thing about it was? No one knew anything about it.

The first week or so was horrible. My tummy kept rumbling and I got painfully hungry at lunchtime but I eventually worked out that chewing on chewing gum soon satisfied my hunger pangs. I drank lots of juice and chewed lots of chewing gum and that's what kept me going. I ate breakfast and dinner as normal and so no one knew anything about what I was doing with my lunch except me.

This went on for a couple of weeks but it began to get too easy. I needed to do something else. So I decided that I would skip breakfast as well. I would go downstairs half an hour earlier than any one else in my family, put some cereal crumbs along with some milk in a bowl, swish it round a bit, tip it all in the bin and leave my bowl and licked spoon on the kitchen worktop so it looked like I'd had my breakfast.

I remember the first day I did it and I wondered whether anyone would ask any questions or notice any differences. No one noticed a thing. Once again I had got away with it.

This time the first few days were really horrible because I was now skipping breakfast and lunch. My stomach was playing an actual symphony! It was making the strangest noises but I knew that all it took was a few pieces of chewing gum and a drink of water and it would soon settle down. It was almost as if I was playing a little game with my own mind – like I was on a power trip against myself. If I was able to maintain control, be determined and not give in it meant that I was a strong, powerful and controlled human being . . . or so I thought.

This went on for a number of weeks but by this time people were starting to comment and ask questions.

I remember being in the music room at school and my friend Tommy made a remark about how he never saw me eating anything at lunchtime. I made up some feeble excuse and brushed it off. People were coming up to me and complimenting me on how good I looked. Not only was I in control but people were also approving of me.

I secretly quite liked the fact that a few people like Tommy were noticing because it meant that I had to be really careful about what I allowed other people to see. It meant that I had to be even more secretive. It wasn't easy any more. This was going to take guts and determination and I was prepared to do whatever it took to complete my mission.

I was losing weight rapidly and I felt so good about myself. In fact I felt great! I was totally in control and I was luvin' it.

However, internally my body was responding in a very different way. It got to the point after three or four months where I was hardly eating a thing. I tricked people into thinking I was eating breakfast, I threw my packed lunch away and I lied about eating my dinner (or tea as I like to call it). I used every excuse I could possibly think of to get out of eating my tea: 'I'm not hungry', 'I've had tea at my friend's house', 'I feel sick', etc. A lot of the time it worked but sometimes it didn't.

I was constantly plotting and weighing things up in my mind, *How will it look if I do this? Is it too risky if I do that? Will I get away with it if I do this?* Questions endlessly rattled around in my head.

Looking back I guess you have to be pretty intelligent to have an eating disorder with all the deceit and forward thinking that's involved: always being one step ahead; always knowing your next move. Sometimes I had to eat my tea for the sake of satisfying my parents' suspicions but I would always make sure that it never stayed in my stomach for too long. The next day I would ask to go to the toilet during a lesson, usually a maths lesson. I would walk into a toilet cubicle and firmly close the door behind me. I would stay silent for several seconds whilst I listened to see if there was anyone else in the toilets. If there was, I would wait until they had gone. Then I would stick my fingers down my throat and make myself sick.

It was rarely as simple as that, though. I remember the first time I tried to do it and it didn't work – no matter how many times I stuck my fingers down my throat I just couldn't be sick. I would heave and gag but I wasn't sick. I would sit on the cold, brown-tiled floor with my back against the toilet door and just cry. I cried if I wasn't sick and I cried if I was sick. I was totally and utterly confused. I didn't know what was happening to me. This 'thing' that I had started off in control of was actually beginning to control me and I felt powerless. There was nothing that I could do to make it stop. I was addicted to not eating. You hear stories about people who are addicted to drugs; people who are addicted to alcohol; people who are even addicted to having sex. I never thought that anyone could ever be addicted to not eating.

The funny thing is that I distinctly remember reading a magazine article months before this all happened about a young girl who was struggling with an eating disorder. The article included a list of 'things to look out for' in people who were going down the eating-disorders road. I remember thinking to myself, *How can people choose not to eat anything? You must be pretty stupid to make a choice like that.*

Looking back I don't think I ever made a conscious choice to stop eating. It just happened. I never thought in a million years that I would ever find myself walking down that same road. I sometimes wonder whether reading that magazine article influenced me in any way and whether it played a part in me making the choices I made when it came to food. Maybe, maybe not – who knows? All I knew was that I didn't want to walk down that road any more and something had to change.

CHAPTER 4

FOUND OUT

You can't hide from God. There's no where you can run to escape his presence. He's not sat up there in judgement of me... he's stood here beside me, helping me through it.

This situation kept getting gradually worse for about four months. I was eating less and less, the lies were getting bigger and bigger and I eventually found myself eating next to nothing. More and more people were noticing. Family members that hadn't seen me for a while were expressing their concern about my weight.

Even I was noticing a difference. My skin was covered with dry, brown patches due to the lack of vitamins and minerals I was taking in. My hair was in terrible condition. My periods had virtually stopped. I found it difficult to sing and play the piano because I had very little energy. I was tired all the time and had constant headaches. The skin across my stomach would hurt when I stretched because it was being pulled too tight. I remember having my TB injection at school and the needle snapped in my arm because there was hardly any flesh to inject into.

All the while I was convincing myself that there was nothing wrong with me. I used to try and justify every-thing and tell myself that I would be OK, when deep down inside I think I knew that I was in a mess – it's just that I didn't know what to do about it. All of my clothes were too big for me and I liked that because it meant people couldn't see the outline of my body as much. I used to wear baggy t-shirts and baggy trousers in my dance classes because if I were to wear leotards or skin-tight dance clothes like everyone else, people would have been able to see my bones sticking out. The last thing I wanted was for people to be asking me questions and confronting me about my rapid weight loss. I avoid-ed having my picture taken at all costs – the camera and me were not friends!

I remember 'the night' when my mum and dad confronted me about it all. It was a Wednesday evening and my mum had made me some tea. In fact she had made my favourite – cottage pie!

Wednesday night was when I had my keyboard lesson with my teacher, Nick. It was quite easy on a Wednesday to get out of eating my tea because I would sit there for ages just staring at it until Nick came round. Then I would conveniently 'have to leave the dinner table' because Nick had come to give me my lesson. By the time I had finished my lesson my food had gone cold, so I just left it and had nothing. But this Wednesday night was different.

I was sitting at the kitchen worktop on a stool and my mum walked over and put my tea down in front of me. I pushed it away and said, 'I don't want it.'

My mum pushed it back in front of me and said, 'You will sit there until it's gone.'

I pushed it away again and said something along the lines of, 'I don't have to eat it if I don't want to.'

Once again, my mum pushed the plate back in front of me and said, 'Michelle, you will sit there until it's all gone.'

And so I sat there . . . and sat there . . . and sat there. Nick arrived as usual and I went to get off my stool to go to have my lesson. But not this time. This time I was made to stay on the stool . . . no keyboard lesson . . . no nothing. I could see that my mum was serious about this but still I refused to eat.

I was determined to stay in control . . . or at least to hold on to that little bit of control I still had left. Nick came and went. That's when the questions began. See, I didn't know this at the time, but my mum had phoned a helpline and talked to them about my eating habits. My parents asked me all sorts of questions and I was quite happy at this point to tell them the truth. I don't know why. Maybe I sensed defeat and somehow thought that if I told them the truth then I was still in control because I was choosing to tell them what was really going on. They then asked me if I was making myself sick and I said, 'Yes.'

I lay in bed that night wondering what was going to happen next. All sorts of feelings, thoughts, emotions and questions were spinning round and round in my head. I was so confused. It was as if my soul was caught up in someone else's body . . . like I was thinking someone else's thoughts. I didn't have a clue who I was any more. I had lost all sense of purpose. I wasn't in control at all. I used to be in control all those weeks ago when I first decided to throw my packed lunch away . . . but I wasn't in control any more. This 'thing' was in control of me. I couldn't stop it. It was like it had a mind of its own. It was making me think things that deep down I didn't really want to think. It was making me do things that deep down I didn't really want to do. But I just felt completely helpless. I didn't have the energy to fight it any more. I didn't have the energy to do anything.

The next morning I got up and got ready for school. But wait a minute? Something was different. My dad hadn't gone to work. I knew straight away that something was going on.

I ran downstairs and asked Mum what was happening.

'You're not going to school this morning, Michelle.'

Panic struck within me. 'Why? What's going on?' I said quickly.

'Me and your dad are taking you to the doctors,' Mum said.

'But there's nothing wrong with me,' I pleaded.

Mum didn't say anything else. She just carried on making my brother's sandwiches. I remember standing there and feeling as if my whole body had caved in on itself. My stomach sank, my heart sank and it was like I had internally collapsed. As a 15-year-old girl all I could do now was cry and kick and scream – in a very similar way to how I'd cried and kicked and screamed at 5 years old when I couldn't have that dress.

My brother went to school and my mum and dad had to push me down the driveway and into the car. I had certainly lost all power and control now.

We drove to the doctor's surgery a couple of miles away from our house and I sat there in complete silence. I remember walking in and my mum gave my name in at reception. The doctor we were seeing, Dr J (as I used to call him), was situated at the other end of the building. We walked past two or three waiting room areas before we eventually got to Dr J's waiting room. I sat down, picked up a magazine and pretended to read it. I wasn't really reading it – I just didn't want to talk. We sat there for what seemed like hours.

Then Dr J opened his door and said, 'Michelle Whittaker?' All three of us walked into the room and the door was closed behind us.

It was a typical doctor's room painted in two drab-looking colours – white and a bluey-grey – and there was a token pink and blue flowery border that was stuck half way down each wall. As you walked in through the door, Dr J's desk was in the top left corner. There was an examination bed to the right, a window facing the door and a few official-looking chairs were scattered around the room.

The one thing that I liked about Dr J's room was that he had pictures of his family everywhere – on the wall, on his desk. I don't know why I liked it but it somehow made me feel more comfortable; more at home.

I didn't feel very comfortable this time though. I sat on a chair that was near the examination bed. I sat there because it was the chair that was furthest away from all the others. I don't think I had ever felt so alone and so iso-lated in my life. I sat down and wrapped my arms around my tummy as I always did at this point so that no one could see what was underneath – or more to the point what wasn't underneath.

Dr J asked, 'What can I do for you?' From that point on I lost my will to speak. I do tend to have a stubborn streak that flows within me, as does my mum. I think that's why we had so many heated disagreements through my teenage years. When we decide to do something, we do it and we do it well. The same goes for when we decide not to do something and this time I had decided that I was not going to start talking to anyone.

Most of the appointment was taken up by me remaining silent and my mum doing the talking. My mum began telling Dr J about everything that was going on. She told him about me refusing to eat, about me making myself sick, about me losing weight – everything. I sat on my own, still totally convinced that nothing was wrong with me. All I saw were three people sitting in a room, talking about me as if I wasn't there, referring to me as 'she' rather than 'Michelle' and trying their best to convince me that I was ill.

Dr J listened to everything they said. There was a brief silence as three pairs of disheartened eyes glared at me with such disappointment. It was as if there was a silent, patronising message being beamed over to me through their eyes – *Oh dear, Michelle. What are we going to do with you?*

Dr J began to tell me about the pressure that I was putting on my body; how I would have knocked years off my life span due to the pressure that I had put on my heart. He asked me if my periods had stopped. I didn't really say much but I knew that they were now only lasting a day, if that. He told me that by putting pressure on my reproductive system I could have reduced my chances of having children in the future. He then told me the scariest bit of all – that if I didn't start eating again I wouldn't have much more than eight weeks left to live. He asked me whether I was going to start eating again myself or whether I wanted to be admitted to hospital and be force-fed through tubes. I decided that I wanted to try eating myself. I didn't want to kill myself. I didn't stop eating as a way of ending my life. I just wanted to be in control. And for four months I had tried my hardest to be successful at doing just that but I had been defeated. I had failed.

Within a matter of minutes of walking in to Dr J's surgery my world had been shattered. I was being controlled by a disease; a state of mind; a stupid mission. I was leading the mission. I was the one fighting on the front line. I was the one ducking and diving and planning the way ahead, but my mission had been sabotaged. And the scariest part of it all was that my fight hadn't even really begun. Now was the time that I was really going to have to start fighting.

On Thursday, 20 January 2000, I was officially diagnosed as having an eating disorder called anorexia nervosa.

CHAPTER 5

THE ROAD TO RECOVERY

"All your tears for all those years will fall away."

('Sorry and Safe' by tbc – Pennells/Porter)

That afternoon, my parents and I went to the shopping-centre across the road from the doctor's surgery and went to the supermarket to buy me some food. The condition of trying to feed myself was that I chose all of my own food. I filled two baskets full of 'fat free food'. I had fat free bread, skimmed milk, fat free yoghurts and cheese, fat free pasta, fat free cereal – fat free everything. I knew the fat content and nutritional information of every product in my basket and I very quickly became obsessed with what I allowed to pass through my mouth.

I got home and thought, *I know, I'll have a yoghurt.* I took my yoghurt out of the fridge, got a spoon, peeled off the lid, got a spoonful of yoghurt on my spoon and stopped. A hundred thoughts went through my head all at once. *Am I going to put loads of weight on by eating this yoghurt? Where's it going to show on my body? Is it going to make me fat? How many calories does this have in it? Can I really do this?* I knew I had to eat but this was going to be harder than I thought. I waited a while, took a deep breath and ate a spoonful of yoghurt. *There, I've done it,* I told myself. Every spoonful of that yoghurt was the same. It was one of the hardest things I have ever had to do and it took me ages to finish it. I eventually swallowed the last spoonful and I felt full up. I remember asking myself the question, *How can I feel full when I've only had a yoghurt?* What I didn't realise at the time was that when you stop eating for a substantial period of time, your stomach begins to shrink. It gets smaller and smaller and when you start eating again it takes a while for it to go back to its normal size. My stomach had shrunk, which is why I felt full after only eating a yoghurt.

For the next few months, meal times were the worst. I hated being watched by people when I was eating and it frustrated me because no one trusted me any more when it came to food. It would take me ages to eat something and I would feel so sick by the end of it. My whole perception of having a human digestive system went out the window. Instead I would look at whatever it was I was eating and wonder where I was going to see it appear on my body. For example, if I was eating a jacket potato, I would look at it and envisage it appearing under my skin as a whole jacket potato. If I were eating a plate of pasta, I would look at the pasta and imagine it appearing under another part of my skin as a whole plate of pasta. It was as if I had forgotten about my body's ability to take food in, digest it, and use it for whatever it needed to be used for. I would literally sit at the dinner table and cry, not because I didn't want to eat, but because I now wanted to eat and found it so difficult.

The hardest bit of all was trying to talk to the people closest to me about the way I felt and being totally misunderstood. It seemed like no one could understand what I was going through. People tried so hard to understand but they just didn't get it. All I wanted was for someone to grab hold of me and tell me that everything was going to be OK, but no one could do that because no one knew how it was going to end up. I had good days and I had really bad days and that's what my life was like for a long time – a big, unpredictable mess.

I remember my very first counselling appointment at the hospital. It wasn't in the main hospital building; it was in a side building called Guardian House. Mum and Dad parked the car and we all walked over to Guardian House. There was a single door and then a few flights of stairs to climb before you got to the reception desk. I remember walking in through the front door and noticing a sign that said 'Mental Health Unit' with an arrow pointing in the way we were heading. We got to the next set of stairs and there was another identical sign with another arrow pointing in the direction that we were walking. We got to the reception desk and there was a sign on the door saying 'Welcome to the Mental Health Unit'. I was utterly puzzled. Why on earth was I standing in the mental health ward? I didn't have a mental illness! I laughed under my breath and went along with it anyway. Maybe we were in the department that was next to the mental health unit. I gave my name in at reception and we were told to take a seat and wait.

The waiting room was painted blue and lined with blue chairs. There was a typical wooden coffee table in the middle of the room with magazines neatly laid out. There was a play area in the far left corner and the whole room had a very 'child-like' feel to it. Within a few minutes, a small and very fragile-looking lady walked into the room and said, 'Michelle Whittaker?' We all stood up to greet her. The lady shook my hand and we were guided out of the waiting room, down a corridor and into another room that was this time painted in a warm beige colour.

The lady closed the door, sat down and said, 'Hello Michelle, my name's Sheila.'

Everything about Sheila appeared to be fragile. She had a petite frame and very fine, jaw-length, strawberry blonde hair. She had a little face and a delicate voice that spoke out such warmth and comfort. She had a lovely posture and a kind-hearted nature about her. She was just one of those people who you knew really cared.

The next thing I remember was being asked to draw myself on a piece of white paper with some wax crayons. It was at this point that I started to get confused. I knew that a lot of people in my shoes would have drawn themselves as a big fat blob even though they were super skinny but I didn't see myself like that. I didn't know how I saw myself? So I just drew an average sized figure. I remember having to be weighed too . . . I really didn't like being weighed. My target weight to start off with was 8 stone. I was 6½ stone at this point and despised the thought of having to be any heavier. I was weighed every week from then on and I hated it. It made me feel childish and even more ashamed of myself. I was made to stand on the scales in front of everyone with only one layer of clothes on and when the numbers stopped everyone's attention, except mine, was drawn to the final reading. My worst nightmare was having to stand in front of people, see them look me up and down, and then watch their faces change as they saw my pale, skinny, unhealthy body.

I don't really remember anything else from that session apart from being told that I was going to start having counselling sessions every week and that I had to see a dietician (to talk about the best foods to eat and how to achieve a healthy, balanced diet), and a paediatrician (a children's doctor) to monitor my physical health.

I spent quite a bit of time at the hospital each week from then on. I had to keep a diary about what I ate and how I felt. I would often write in it, as it was my way of expressing my emotions and my deepest thoughts. I got to know Sheila quite well and felt that she understood me to a certain extent but wasn't quite 'hitting the nail on the head' so to speak. She was a really lovely lady, though, and I will always appreciate her time and caring ways. I remember asking her early on in our sessions why I had to come to the mental health unit and she replied, 'Because anorexia nervosa is a mental illness.' That was the final straw. I had gone from being a healthy, happy, enthusiastic young woman to being a damaged, unconfident, confused mess all in the space of five months. Was my life ever going to be the same again or had I subconsciously waved goodbye to the Michelle Whittaker that was?

I went back to school and tried my best to act normal – whatever 'normal' was. I was very aware that by now the teachers knew exactly what was going on but I tried to avoid talking about it. I carried on wearing baggy clothes for my dance lessons and I would puff out my shirt so that my frail figure wasn't too noticeable.

I had suddenly become very sensitive about anything to do with weight or size. If it was mentioned in any way I would feel myself bubbling up with anger and fear inside. I did not want to know what people thought when it came to that topic of conversation, and I would pretend not to listen if it was talked about. I couldn't help but listen, though, because there was a raging battle going on within me and I knew what it felt like to struggle with yourself. I knew what it felt like to wake up in the morning, look at yourself in the mirror and be overwhelmed by disappointment. I knew what it felt like to feel ashamed and guilty and know that the only person to blame was you. I knew what it felt like to be lost, as if you'd been taken over by someone or something you didn't know and you were left sitting in a corner feeling totally invisible.

As I look back now, those first few weeks were a daze. It was as if I was floating or being carried through life because someone somewhere knew that was the only way I could cope with what was happening.

CHAPTER 6

A REVELATION

THAT TRAUMA YOU FACED
  WAS NOT EASY,
AND GOD WEPT THAT IT HURT YOU SO;
BUT IT WAS ALLOWED,
  TO SHAPE YOUR HEART,
SO THAT INTO HIS LIKENESS YOU'D GROW

(by Russell Kelfer)

Our assemblies at school were rubbish. They were so dull and boring. Three hundred of us would be ushered in to the assembly hall; members of staff would stand there as if they were hawks, watching us and the state of our uniform. You could be 50 metres away from the hall entrance and all you would hear was, 'Tuck your shirt in!' 'Sort your tie out!' 'Roll your skirt down!' 'Take your jacket off!' 'Why have you got trainers on?' 'Go and wash that muck of your face!' We would walk in, sit down in silence, listen to a ream of notices and then be dismissed and sent to our next lesson.

There are, however, two assemblies that stick in my head from my time at school. The first is Mr Sutton's infamous assembly when I was in Year 9. As usual we were ushered into the hall and made to walk past the 'Bridgewater Hawks' but this time it was different. Instead of hearing the uniform commands from 50 metres away, we heard the sound of the grand piano being played. Everyone walked with a hint of excitement in their step. As we walked through the entrance Mr Sutton was playing the piano. It was a piece from the musical *Carousel*.

Now there are a few things you should know about Mr Sutton. He was a mad science teacher in every sense of the word. I hated science at school but I loved Mr Sutton's physics classes – not because of what we did but because of the way he made us laugh. He was tall with glasses and grey hair, and he would always wear a short-sleeved shirt with a dickey bow. He was a fantastic teacher! Anyway . . . back to the assembly.

So, 300 students are sitting in the assembly hall with smiles beginning to appear as we watch Mr Sutton play the piano. All of us are sitting there wondering, 'What's this all about?' Well . . . you'll never guess what happened next! Mr Sutton got up from the piano and started roller-skating frantically around the assembly hall! By this point we were all in hysterics. There was not one person who wasn't laughing their head off. To be perfectly honest, I can't really remember what the assembly was about . . . I think it was something along the lines of 'knowing what you're good at' or 'using your talents'. The reason I remember it so well is because it was totally unexpected and it was one of the few times I laughed in a school assembly.

The second assembly, or group of assemblies, I remember were the ones that Steve did. Steve was a youth worker at Bridgewater High School and worked for a charity called Warrington Youth For Christ (WYFC). We had a WYFC assembly probably every month or so and the majority of students looked forward to them. When you walked through the entrance and saw that Steve was doing the assembly you would breathe a sigh of relief because you knew it was going to be good and not at all boring. The way Steve's assemblies worked was this: he would do a game, an icebreaker of some sort, and then relate the game or icebreaker to a verse from the Bible. He would then talk for a few minutes about it and leave us all with a challenge. He talked about things like 'treating other people as you would want to be treated', 'respecting those around you', 'speaking well of others' . . . just all-round good, morally correct issues. Then at Christmas and Easter he would do assemblies that talked about the Christian message but were fun at the same time.

Steve didn't just do assemblies in our school, he also took part in RE (Religious Education) lessons and was around at breaks and lunchtimes just making himself available for light chats or deep conversations. He would split his time between lower site and upper site and he was always very open about what he believed as a Christian. Some people liked him for that and some people didn't, but that was who he was and the majority of people just accepted it.

I remember one particular day, a few months before I had been diagnosed with having an eating disorder, when I came across Steve in the upper school entrance hall. It was still relatively early on in the new academic year and I had stopped eating and was beginning to feel really rubbish about myself. We began to chat and suddenly, out of nowhere, six words came out of his mouth that just made me stop in disbelief: 'Shell, God loves you so much.'

I didn't know whether to laugh or cry but I just remember feeling really angry inside. In the space of a split second I remember thinking, *How insensitive! How can you say that God loves me when he's allowing me to go through such crap.* But I don't think that's what came across on the outside because I soon found myself being drawn to what Steve had said. We moved to the side of the entrance hall and stood in front of a notice board that was displayed above a warming radiator. Steve kept on talking and every so often I heard him say, 'Shell, God loves you so much.' He kept on saying things like, 'You're special' and 'You're loved' and 'You're precious'. But I didn't feel special or loved or precious. I felt like I was in a mess that I was really struggling to cope with. I felt too ashamed and too guilty to be loved by anyone, let alone God. And anyway, I thought God was supposed to be this all-powerful, all-loving, all-knowing, ever-present God. That's what I'd been told in my RE lessons. I thought God was supposed to be kind and caring and comforting; I thought he was supposed to bring peace and hope. I didn't feel any of those things so how could God love me? Was God even real? Before I could say anything in response to all of these strange and unfamiliar words, Steve opened his Bible and began to read a verse to me from Revelation, the last book of the Bible. This is what it said

> 'Look! I stand at the door and knock. If you hear my voice and open the door, I will come in, and we will share a meal together as friends.'

(Revelation 3:20)

Oh great, so not only is this guy telling me that God loves me, he's also telling me that Jesus wants to share some food with me. How insensitive considering I'm not eating at the moment!

This thought-out conversation in my head was so real but I couldn't muster up the strength to say anything – and anyway I didn't want to drop any clues about my 'secret situation'. So I just nodded my head and hoped our little chat would come to an end soon.

The bell rang to signal the end of lunchtime and I thanked Steve and walked to my next class. The strange thing was that I just couldn't seem get those words that Steve had spoken out of my head. I tried to forget about them but I couldn't. They just kept going round and round as if they were being played continuously on a tape reel in my mind.

That's pretty much all I remember from our conversation that day. One thing I do know is that I will never forget it and I will always be grateful to Steve for caring enough to spend a little bit of time with me and letting me know that at least someone loved me when I felt completely unlovable.

Now I just want to rewind a little further back to a few weeks before my chat with Steve in the entrance hall. I had chosen to study music as one of my GCSEs and the music room at upper site was amazing! The whole room was lined with computers so that you could use the music software programs. There were tables in the middle of the room and there was a beautiful electronic piano on the left as you walked in. I loved spending my break and lunchtimes playing the piano and writing songs.

I'd only been in Year 10 and at this new site for a couple of weeks at this point. I was playing the piano during a particular lunch break when the music room door creaked opened and in walked one of the sixth formers (or college students – whatever you prefer to call them). As soon as I saw him I knew that I knew him from somewhere. I didn't say anything. He just walked in, got something and walked out. Then it clicked. *I'm sure I used to be in a choir with that guy* I told myself but I carried on playing the piano and thought nothing of it.

A few days later I was playing the piano in the music room again when the door creaked open and in walked the same guy. This time I asked him, 'Do I know you from somewhere?'

He replied by saying, 'I don't know.'

'I'm sure I know you . . . did we used to be in a choir together?' I asked.

'I don't know.'

I continued by asking the most ridiculous and random question ever, 'Did your mum used to drive a brown Volvo?'

He looked at me in weird kinda way, 'Yeah, she did.'

I can't remember whether it was that time or the next time I saw him but I found out that his name was Jon. I saw Jon in the music room almost every day after that and I quickly realised that I quite liked him – in fact I liked him a lot if you get what I mean! I also found out that he went to church and was very good friends with Steve. They were in a band together called Under Scrutiny. What a bizarre coincidence! It all seemed to come at just the right time. Jon was the only one who knew anything about the fact that I was struggling with eating. For some unknown reason I felt that I could confide in him. I by no means told him everything but he knew quite a bit. He knew more about me than a lot of people at that time and because of that I felt like there was a connection between us.

One day Jon asked me if I wanted to go and watch his band rehearse at the local church. I said yes, waited until he had gone out of the room and then began to uncontrollably giggle to myself. Jon had asked me if I wanted to go and watch his band rehearse! I had to pinch myself. *For goodness sake, get a grip woman. He's only invited you to his band practice . . . it's not a date . . . there are going to be other people there you know!* It didn't matter how many times I told myself that very thing. I still got excited.

I arrived at the church that was approximately two and a half miles away from my house. It was a little church on a hill called Hillcliffe Baptist Church. It didn't look much like a church. There was no steeple, no wrought iron front door, no red carpet, no grand sandstone bricks – nothing. It was an average-sized brick building with an entrance hall, a church hall to the left and the main church sanctuary to the right. I walked into the main church bit and saw several rows of pews, organ pipes, a few intricate stained glass windows and a raised platform where Jon and Steve were setting up their instruments. Jon was setting up his guitar and mic stand and Steve was setting up his drums. We all said hello and I sat on one of the wooden pews in the middle of the room.

As we were chatting another guy walked in. I remember looking at his face and then realising what he was wearing. He was wearing a plain white t-shirt and then, oh no . . . surely not . . . oh my goodness . . . is he for real? Yep . . . he was wearing green, yellow and blue chequered MC Hammer pants that were overly baggy at the top and tighter round the ankles. I remember thinking to myself, *He's got a lovely smile but, oh my word, what is he wearing?!* He was dragging a dark red, rectangular case behind him.

Jon said, 'This is Tim, our keyboard player.'

'Nice to meet you, Tim. I'm Shell.' (By this point I had been renamed Shell. Only my mum and dad called me Michelle.)

I sat there for well over an hour and watched them rehearse. They sounded pretty good and the songs were really catchy. I remember feeling a little worried when Jon told me that Under Scrutiny was a Christian band that practised in a church. I had this vision of it being more like a cheesy church worship group who sung songs about condemnation, rather than a rock band who had quite a bit of credibility – I was actually very impressed.

It was funny you know . . . I felt strangely drawn to Jon, Steve and Tim but I didn't know why. They were all older than me, they were very different to me yet they seemed to take me under their wings – not in a weird way, just in a lovely way. I began to see them every week because they asked me if I wanted to join the band as a backing singer and I'd accepted their invitation. The thing I loved about them was that they were all so real. I met a few of Jon's other friends and they were the same. They were kind and funny and caring and they seemed to accept me for who I was, even though I didn't believe in God like they did. I had never experienced that before. I had never been in any sort of relationship where I could just be me. They broke every stereotype I had of what being a Christian and going to church was all about. They weren't wackos who bashed you over the head with a Bible – they were normal, down-to-earth, real people.

I remember telling Jon, Steve and Tim about the fact that I had an eating disorder. Most of the people I told were family members and even though they tried to disguise it, I could quite clearly see the disappointment in their eyes. I'll never forget that day when I sat in Dr J's surgery with my arms tightly wrapped around my tummy. I saw my mum and dad fall to pieces inside when they were told I had an eating disorder and potentially had eight weeks left to live. I saw the shame and the fear and the shock in their faces as they had to come to terms with their daughter's failings. That's what I felt like – a fraud and a failure. I was worried about telling Jon, Steve and Tim. But they were really supportive and I remember them asking me if I would mind them praying for me. Well I couldn't say no could I?! I can't remember what they prayed but I remember feeling really peaceful afterwards. There was something different about these three people but I couldn't quite put my finger on it.

CHAPTER 7

THE ULTIMATE DIFFERENCE

"So, if you're serious about living this new resurrection life with Christ, act like it. Pursue the things over which Christ presides. Don't shuffle along, eyes to the ground, absorbed with the things right in front of you. Look up and be alert to what is going on around Christ – that's where the action is. See things from his perspective."
(Colossians 3v1-2 – The Message Bible)

It was February 2000. By this time I had been diagnosed with anorexia for about a month. Life was simply ticking along and the whole 'food issue' was still a big hurdle. Some days it felt slightly easier and other days were really hard, but I was beginning to feel like I had a support network around me. I was having weekly counselling sessions and I had discussed my diet with the dietician at great length. I was still struggling to eat solid food but I was having supplement milkshakes and build-up drinks. They contained lots of essential vitamins and minerals, so I was starting to feel a bit better in myself. The brown patches on my skin were slowly disappearing, I was feeling slightly more energetic and I was taking little pin steps towards my goal of recovery. It would be like that for a few days and then I would have a really bad day and almost have to start all over again. I just took it one day at a time and tried to remain patient.

I had also realised by now that I really really really liked Jon and very much wanted to be his girlfriend. We saw each other most days and became really good friends. I remember a particular day he wasn't in school. I got really worried and sent him a text message asking him if he was OK. It turned out that he had been in hospital to have his appendix out. I dropped everything I was doing and went to visit him after school. He was lying on his mum's sofa, drugged up and feeling sorry for himself. I was glad I could be there to comfort him, just as he'd been there to comfort me over the previous few months.

He came back to school after a week or so. The tiered staging had gone up in the hall for a performance that was about to take place. Bridgewater had special Arts College status so there were always lots of shows and plays going on. The grand piano had been moved into the corner of the hall. I remember there being a day when there was lots of hustle and bustle. People were dashing round and making lots of noise and Jon and I just sat talking underneath the grand piano. I forget exactly what was said but I do know it was an extremely significant conversation about where I stood when it came to God.

Where did I stand when it came to God? I had still not managed to get the words that Steve had said to me in the entrance hall out of my head. Jon had said similar things to me about how he believed God loved me and thought I was really valuable. Being in Under Scrutiny had taught me loads about God. I didn't really understand any of it but it sounded good!

I went home that night and I sat on my bed. I had never really prayed before, apart from crisis prayers and going through the stage of 'praying to the moon' but that was just a load of old gobbledygook. I closed my eyes and I simply said, 'God, if you love me as much as these people are saying that you love me, then you need to come and help me because I'm in a mess and I don't really know what to do.'

I opened my eyes in anticipation of what was going to happen next. Nothing happened. I somehow had this expectation that maybe life would get a little bit easier . . . or maybe the grass would grow a little bit greener . . . or maybe there would be rainbows and blue skies that would follow me wherever I went. There was no big, booming voice, no clouds parted – nothing. I just felt still and peaceful. But there was one thing that felt different – I felt an overwhelming sense of love. I somehow knew in the depths of my heart that I was accepted and valued. I felt, for the first time in a long, long time, that I was actually worth something. I knew what it felt like to be unconditionally loved and the only thing I could put it down to was God. But why would God want to love me? I mean I'd spent the previous five months telling blatant lies; I'd done a whole host of things wrong before that; and I had spent fifteen years not wanting to know him – why on earth would God choose to reveal his love to me? All I know is that I didn't understand it in my head but I definitely felt it in my heart.

My relationship with Jon flourished and we ended up becoming an official 'item'. I continued to have counselling sessions with Sheila at the hospital and she said she had noticed a real difference in me. I started attending Hillcliffe Baptist Church on a regular basis and I even made the decision to get baptised. I made lots of new friends, both in school and outside of school, and most of them had commented on the fact that they had seen a difference in me too.

My eating habits were slowly improving. I still hated people watching me eat and I occasionally had really bad days, but I was getting closer and closer to my target weight and I was beginning to have a spring in my step again. I wasn't getting bullied at school and I wasn't having to have as many supplement drinks because I was now eating enough solid food. Within the space of a year my life had been completely transformed and I felt like a new person. The old Michelle had gone and been replaced by the new Shell, who spent the vast majority of her time simply loving life, laughing out loud, and making the most of things.

What was it that had made the difference? What turned that little bulb on in my head? What was it that gave me a reason to fight and get my life back? Was it family? Was it friends? Was it treatment at the hospital? I think it's safe to say that it was probably a mixture of all three. But there was one other thing – or person, if you like – who I knew had made the ultimate difference . . . God.

You see, I had been told when I was first diagnosed with having an eating disorder, 'Once an anorexic always an anorexic.' Millions of people suffer from some sort of eating disorder and many of them never fully recover. It ends up being something that they carry around with them for the rest of their lives, almost like a security blanket I suppose. I feel incredibly blessed to be able to sit here and say that by March 2003, three years and two months after I had been diagnosed with it, having an eating disorder of any kind was no longer an issue for me. I had experienced God's love and his healing power in a real and undeniable way. I used to be really sceptical about whether or not God could heal people – I used to wonder whether or not he even existed – but the more I went to church and the more I read my Bible, the more I wanted to know God and the more I believed he existed. My faith grew like wildfire in a very short space of time.

I like to think of it like this: when someone gives you a gift, the thing to do is accept it and say thank you. You don't throw it back in their face or complain about it, you just receive it. The chances are that you will never receive a gift from a stranger – gifts are usually from people who know you and love you. Well, I believe that the day I sat on my bed and asked God to help me, he gave me a very special gift – a gift of love – and I chose to accept that gift with a thankful heart. The difference is that I didn't know the Giver of that gift and I decided that I wanted to get to know him more. That's why I started to go to church. If someone loves me enough to give me such a personal and priceless gift then I want to get to know that person and find out why he loves me and how he knows me. And that's what I did.

Three years and two months sounds like a long time. I was actually discharged from the hospital a long time before that . . . around about June or July 2001, I think. I was fine for a long time. I ate normally, had a great appetite (after all, I had to make up for lost time!) and never once tried to make myself sick. But then, fifteen months or so after that, I relapsed a little and began trying to make myself sick again. I remember it came to a head when I went to visit Tim one time at university.

Oh . . . I almost forgot to tell you . . . Jon and I went out for eighteen months, February 2000 to August 2001, and then went our separate ways. Four months after that, Tim and I (the keyboard player from Under Scrutiny) started going out. Then we split up . . . and then we got back together again . . . it's complicated, I know!

Tim went to a university in Manchester to study engineering and lived in a massive house in Withington, Manchester with a handful of other people. I went to visit Tim at his house in Withington. His room was next to the bathroom on the very top floor of the house. I went to use the toilet and fell to pieces on the floor next to the toilet. I don't really understand, to this day, what happened.

What I do know is how I felt. I felt as if there was a physical battle going on within me. Tears were rolling down my face as I sat beside the toilet. Half of me was trying to make myself sick and the other half of me was trying to stop myself. My mind was playing games with me.

Eventually I found the strength to flush the toilet, wash my hands and face, walk into Tim's room and fall into his arms in a big, teary-eyed heap. He held me, for what seemed like hours, as I cried about what had just happened and the turmoil that was going on within me. That was when I realised I had to do something about it. I had got over it once before and I could do it again.

At the beginning of 2003 I went to see a private psychiatric counsellor, called Carol, in Liverpool. You see, I had been discharged from the hospital and I had been coping really well on my own, but I still didn't understand what had really happened. I needed to understand why I had suffered from an eating disorder. I needed to delve into my inner being and ask questions like why, what, how and when? I needed to be able to put to bed everything that had happened to me and I couldn't do that until I had had a few questions answered.

I will go as far as saying that those six or eight sessions with Carol totally changed my perspective on life. I came away with more from those sessions than I did from eighteen months of counselling at the hospital. Why? Because I now felt that I understood and knew myself a whole lot better. I discovered during those sessions that food meant way more to me than I thought it did and food satisfied so many things within me; food to me was something that I could trust; something that wouldn't talk back at me or bully me. Food was something that I could be in control of and hide away in. Food enabled me to be everything I wanted to be.

It sounds crazy, I know, but it was true for me at that point in my life. There were even certain types of food that I was more drawn to than others: cheese, chocolate and yoghurt. When I was discharged from the hospital I was eating almost everything. If ever I felt down in the dumps I would look to food for comfort, and guess what I would eat: cheese, chocolate or a yoghurt. I learnt so much about my character and my identity in those sessions and that is what I was missing. I needed to know who I was again so that I could make sure I didn't become someone I didn't want to be, if that makes any sense at all.

I never set out to become an 'anorexic' . . . it wasn't a goal of mine to be a size zero. I just had so much stuff going on in my life and so much emotional baggage from things that had happened in the past. I was a 15-year-old girl who didn't know how to cope. I didn't know this at the time but anorexia was my way of dealing with it all and covering up my pain. Some people hide their pain by turning to drink or drugs. Some people think that having sex and being made to feel 'special' will sort it all out. Some people become addicted to shopping or buying things and they try to find their worth in material possessions. Others simply stay silent and torture themselves with guilt and regret for the rest of their lives. My personal opinion is that the best way to get through something is to deal with it as soon as possible. It may be difficult and uncomfortable and it may take time but it's better than allowing it to take a portion of your life away. Deep inside you can find the strength to do something about it. I'm living proof that it's possible.

Carol helped me to re-live my past so that I could discover my future. The end of those sessions symbolised the end of the road when it came to me having an eating disorder. I could now live in freedom, knowing what to look out for when it came to food and having the emotional tools to deal with it.

'Once an anorexic, always an anorexic' – how wrong they were.

THE NEW ME

CHAPTER 8

THE CALL

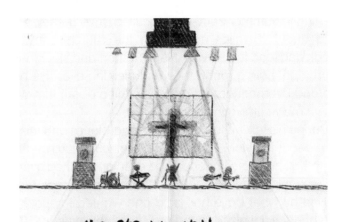

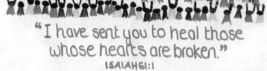

"I have sent you to heal those whose hearts are broken."

ISAIAH 61:1

I want to take you back to Summer 2000. I would describe the year 2000 as a year when I built the foundations for my new life. People at school would often ask me, 'Are you religious?' My answer was, 'I don't think Christianity is about being part of a religion . . . it's about being in a relationship with God.' My relationship with God was growing day by day and I considered him to be an essential part of my life. Church for me was not about turning up, singing songs, hearing sermons and meeting people. It was (and still is) about worshipping and experiencing God, learning more about him and being with like-minded people who believe the same thing as you.

I remember a significant church service on a Sunday evening in Summer 2000. A guy called Dave Tierney, who lived about 10 miles away from the church, came to speak and lead the service. He was short and stocky with short, dark hair, a round face and piercing eyes. He had a broad Liverpool accent and everything about him was awesomely captivating.

During his talk he told some personal stories and talked a lot about the Holy Spirit. Like after all our church services, the kitchen hatch opened and everyone rushed over to get a cup of tea and a biscuit! But I didn't. I was really moved by what Dave had said and wanted to speak to him about it. I walked round the church building trying to find Dave and eventually found him standing outside. He was talking to someone else and so I just stood near him and politely waited for him to finish his conversation.

Eventually I got to speak to him and I asked him if he would mind praying for me. My friend Jess was there, too, and so she also prayed for me. All I remember was opening my eyes and seeing Dave staring at me. His eyes showed love and warmth along with great power and authority. He very gently said, 'God has called you to be a healer of broken hearts. Your purpose in this life is to heal broken hearts.' Then he added, 'But don't just rely on me saying that to you . . . ask God to confirm it.'

Man, was I freaked out! What on earth was all that supposed to mean? Here I was, standing outside a church that I'd been attending for six months and some-one, who I've never met before, tells me that God wants me to be a healer of broken hearts. What was I supposed to do with that?!

I remember rushing home and going up to my bed-room. I sat on my bed and thought about how God was going to confirm what I had just been told. I was new to all this and didn't have a clue where to start, so I just thought, *Right, I'll pick up my Bible, let it open on a random page and see what it says.* So that's what I did. I picked up my heavy, silver-covered Bible, closed my eyes, flicked through and let it stop on a random page. All of a sudden, my eyes were drawn to a verse that seemed to jump out at me. It was Isaiah 61:1 and it said, 'He has sent me to comfort those whose hearts are broken.'

My heart skipped a beat and I took in a short, sharp breath. I was absolutely astounded. What had just hap-pened? I remember feeling a sense of excitement bub-bling up within me. My mind was whizzing around and I literally felt like jumping around the room and whooping!

I went to bed that night wondering what it meant to be a healer of broken hearts but decided that if God had said this to me then he would take the lead and some-how show me what it meant. I didn't have to worry because God was now in control!

I left Bridgewater High School in June 2001 and had a really long summer to look forward to. I felt as free as a bird! Mum and Dad had started getting a lot better at the whole 'letting go' thing and I had got a little part-time job at a pharmacy in Stockton Heath village. Mum, Dad and Craig went away on the annual Whittaker two-week holiday to Coniston in the Lake District and I was left with the house to myself . . . it was amazing! I was a very good girl and didn't have any wild parties but I did invite quite a few friends round for DVD nights and takeaways. I was sweet sixteen and enjoying life again. Everything seemed too perfect to be true.

I was enjoying singing and writing songs more than ever. I'd been having singing lessons in school with a lady called Sue and had lots of opportunities through school to perform. I'd written songs for the school play and was writing songs of my own but they had started to follow a different theme. The songs I was writing were no longer about me and my 'issues' – they were about God and the difference he had made to my life. I still have the scruffy bits of paper with the chords and lyrics written on. I occasionally look through them to make sure I've not over looked a number one hit anywhere (!) and some of them make me laugh so much. Talk about cheesy . . . I don't think I've ever seen such terrible lyrics in my life! But they were written from the heart and they meant something to me at the time. Singing and writing songs was my way of expressing my deepest thoughts and emotions. When I opened my mouth to sing, it felt like I was doing what I was made to do. I felt free and at home with myself. I would sit for hours at my keyboard just playing and singing, letting my heart guide my fingers across the black and white keys and simply waiting to see what happened next. It was magical.

And that's when I suddenly realised . . . I want to use my music to heal broken hearts. I want to write and sing songs that are going to help people in whatever circumstances they may be facing in their lives. I want to write lyrics that people will hear and be able to relate to. I want to sing songs that will give hope to people who feel utterly hopeless. And, more than anything, I want to write songs that will reflect God's love in a very real and relevant way.

One thing you should know about me is that I'm a dreamer. I dream up big dreams and think of ways to make them happen. When I get an idea in my head I run with it and become consumed by it – in a healthy way of course! I'm determined and ambitious and I love to take risks – even when other people sometimes try to stop me. Once or twice I've found myself at a dead end and realised that it's not going to happen but most of the time it's ended up being amazing. After all, I would like to be remembered as being someone who had tried and failed, rather than as someone who never tried at all . . . wouldn't you?

So, with my proactive hat on, I decided to raise money to record a demo CD. I wanted to have four or five songs that were recorded professionally so that I could send a demo CD out to some record companies. I told my church leader what I wanted to do and he gave me a five-minute slot in one of our Sunday morning services to stand at the front and tell the church congregation about what I wanted to do. I had done my homework and worked out that

I had to raise £500 per song. I wanted to do at least four songs so that meant raising £2,000. Wow! How was I ever going to do that?

I had spent quite a lot of time praying about it and I really sensed that this was something I had to do . . . so I did it. I stood at the front of my church and said I needed to raise £2,000 to record a demo CD. I sat back in my seat when I had finished and thought, *This is never going to happen. Not in a million years!*

At the end of the service the majority of people rushed to the kitchen hatch for their weekly dose of tea and biscuits, and I sat there wondering whether anyone was going to respond to my plea at the front. To my astonishment, within a few weeks I had enough money to record my first song and promises of more money to come. I could hardly believe it! It just goes to show that prayer really does work.

I recorded my first demo song 'Do You Know What You Believe?' at a little studio in Warrington with a guy called Dave Healey. He was my music teacher's husband and a very talented music producer. I loved every minute of it! I had been in a recording studio quite a few times before but this was amazing! I was recording my own song – surely nothing could get any better than this? Then another £500 came in and I recorded another song called 'Afraid'. Later another £500 was donated and I recorded my third song called 'I Believe' (the cheesiest song in the entire universe!) and I then recorded my fourth song, 'Walk Away'.

I put the songs onto a CD and made a number of copies. I remember sitting at my mum and dad's dining

Baby Shell . . . pretty cute, eh!

My lovely Mum and Dad.

Me and my 'BIG' little brother, Craig.

The terrible twos in 1986.

Looking pretty in pink.

My year 7 high school photo.

Tim, Steve, Me and Jon, true rock 'n' roll in Under Scrutiny.

The very first innervation schools band.

Me and my gorgeous hubby on our wedding day.

My new family – Charlie dog, Emma, Alison, Tim, John
(back) and me.

The tbc ladies in 2005.

Preaching at a tbc gig on the innervation Tour.

The photo shoot for my album, Have You Heard?

Me in Martha's Vineyard, 2008.

table surrounded by CDs in padded envelopes. What on earth was I supposed to do now? I hadn't really thought it through too well, had I? I'd done what I thought was the hard bit in raising £2,000 to record the songs but what good is that if I don't know who to send them to?

I sat down and thought about it a little more logically. I turned the computer on and logged on to the Internet. I decided to get Google's help and typed in 'Christian record labels'. I clicked on the search button and waited a few seconds. As you can probably imagine there were quite a few links that appeared. I searched through them and wrote down a list of about seven record companies. Some were in America and a couple of them were in the UK. I put my demo CD and a letter explaining who I was inside the padded envelopes, sealed them, wrote the addresses on the front and then prayed – hard! I walked to the post box round the corner from my parents' house and hesitantly pushed them in.

As I was pushing them in I had a brief moment of doubt. Did I really want to do this? Was I ready for it? What if no one wrote back to me and I had to deal with the rejection? What if someone did write back to me . . . what was I going to do? I was only 16. I had very little life experience, no money, I couldn't drive, and I was totally dependant on my parents. Was this just a stupid moment of madness? But by the time I had made sense of all the questions it was too late – my demo CDs were comfortably lying at the bottom of the post box and there wasn't a lot I could do about it.

I walked home and wondered what the outcome was going to be. I waited and waited and waited . . . and waited some more. But every day I checked the mail and there was nothing. No letters saying they liked it, no letters saying they didn't like it . . . nothing. Sure I was disappointed but hey at least I had tried and, like I said before, I'd rather die knowing that I had tried and failed than never having tried at all.

So I got on with my life hoping that God knew what he was doing and that all that time, money and effort hadn't gone to waste. By this point I'd started studying performing arts, music and media studies for my A-levels at Bridgewater's sixth form college. I absolutely loved college. It was the best! I loved the subjects I was studying, I had loads of friends, I got on well with my teachers . . . life was good!

My seventeenth birthday came and went and, before I knew it, college was finishing for Christmas.

CHAPTER 9

DECISION TIME

"Be brave and strong! The Lord your God
will always be at your side, and he will
never abandon you." (Deuteronomy 31:6)

I was really looking forward to going back to college in January 2002. On that first day back I had the biggest smile on my face and I got back into the swing of things really quickly. On Wednesday, 23 January, I got home from college and there was a letter waiting for me on the kitchen worktop. I eventually got round to opening it and I was utterly speechless (which for me is an extremely rare occurrence!). Here is a copy of the letter I received. You can read it for yourself.

21st January 2002

Dear Michelle,

Thank you for sending me a copy of your CD entitled 'Do You Know What You Believe' which I have now had an opportunity to listen to, sorry I have taken a while to respond.

I enjoyed your well presented recording, you have a good voice and I thought the song was very good both musically and lyrically. Unfortunately, Alliance are not in a position to offer you anything from a recording point of view at present but I have taken the liberty of forwarding your CD onto a Christian colleague called Mark Pennells as I think he may be interested in what he hears. Mark has worked with The World Wide Message Tribe, Shine and V*enna and he is always on the look out for committed young Christians who have a passion to serve God through music. Please keep doing as much live work as possible, which will help you gain experience.

Thank you for giving Alliance the opportunity to consider the CD and I wish you success in the future so that many more people can enjoy your music and be encouraged.

Yours very sincerely

David Bruce
Marketing Director
cc. Mark Pennells

I could not believe it. I ran to my mum and dad, shoved the letter in front of them and squealed! I had seen The World Wide Message Tribe (TWWMT), Shine and V*enna at concerts I'd been to and they were amazing! I couldn't believe that I'd sent my demo CDs off in the post months ago and now someone had finally got back to me. I remember showing Tim (who was still my boyfriend) the letter and he recognised the name Mark Pennells. We went to his house and he pulled out an old tape cassette from a plastic bag. It was a tape with songs on by TWWMT and on the back was Mark Pennells' autograph. Then, Tim got out a CD he had that was full of Christian pop songs. He looked inside the CD cover at the name of the songwriters and, sure enough, the songs were written by Pennells/Porter. I remember running round the room shouting, 'Oh my goodness! Oh my goodness!'

I eventually calmed down after getting to grips with the reality that it was only a letter. I hadn't been offered a record contract or anything close to that, but at least it was a very encouraging step in the right direction. All I had to do now was wait and see if I heard anything from this Mark Pennells guy . . . but if he took as long as Alliance had taken to get back to me, then I was going to be waiting a while!

Once again, I carried on as normal and spent most of my time working hard at college. But wait . . . something was different. Something felt like it wasn't quite right. I didn't feel excited about going to college any more. At first I just shrugged it off and got on with things as normal but this uneasy feeling wasn't going away. It kept on getting worse. So I prayed and asked God to somehow tell me what was going on. All of a sudden, I got a really strong sense that God was asking me to leave college. *That can't be right*, I said to myself. I ignored it and carried on praying. A few minutes later I sensed it again but this time it was even stronger. It was as if God was standing in the midst of my mind whispering, 'Shell, I want you to leave college.'

OK . . . now I was really freaked out. Why on earth would God want me to leave college? I was having the best time of my life. I had never ever felt so content. What was he playing at?

Despite all of these questions, I decided to go a bit further with it and found myself saying to God, 'OK then. If I were to leave college, what would I be leaving to do? Surely you wouldn't just ask me to leave without telling me what happens next?'

I waited for a while and then heard God's gentle whisper again, 'Shell, I want you to leave college.'

This was getting ridiculous. Never before had I experienced anything so wacky. Was God actually having a laugh?! I stopped praying and decided that none of what had just happened was real . . . after all . . . it was probably just my imagination playing games with me and it didn't seem to make any sense.

After a few days I began to feel sick. Every morning, Monday through to Friday, I would wake up and start feeling sick as soon as I got out of bed. It didn't happen at the weekends – just on the days I went to college. I felt uncomfortable and twitchy when I was in my classes and this feeling of sickness wasn't going away. When I got home from college I felt absolutely fine but then I would wake up the next morning and the whole thing would start again. I blamed it on everything I could possibly think of – my friends, my lessons, my teachers, my family . . . everything. This happened for a few weeks until I reached the point where I couldn't take it any more. I shouted at God and said, 'What on earth is going on? This just isn't funny any more.'

I heard God's gentle whisper once again, 'Shell, I want you to leave college.'

Oh my goodness! This was now beyond a joke. I breathed a deep breath, sat down and tried to think about it logically. *OK . . . so God wants me to leave college but he's not going to tell me what to do after I've left college.* Questions went through my mind like, *Is this me thinking all of this up? . . . How can it be God speaking to me? . . . Am I going insane?* Then I asked the most dangerous question of all . . . *What if God really is asking me to leave college?*

I was very confused, so I thought I'd ask a few older and wiser people at church about it all. They really helped me to understand that God does speak to people but in different ways. Sometimes it's through reading the Bible; sometimes it's through our conscience; God can speak to you through other people or through a poem or a song; sometimes people literally experience the whole 'audible voice' thing.

As I mentioned before, I'm not the sort of person who likes playing it safe. What fun do you get in life if you're not prepared to take any risks? I thought about everything that had been said and everything that had happened very carefully and made one of the most dangerous decisions of my life – to leave college at the end of the school year. That was the easy bit. I now had to find a way of telling my parents. That was going to be very interesting!

Now, there are a few things you should know about the situation with me and my parents at this point. Even though I would say that I wasn't brought up in a Christian home, my mum and dad both had some kind of belief in God. However, when I started going to church and found God for myself, they developed this crazy idea in their heads that I was part of some weird and wonderful cult. You see, the church I went to was very lively and charismatic and my parents were a lot more traditional when it came to their experience of church. I am a very passionate person and when I get involved with anything I throw my whole self into it, not just a little bit of me. So here I was, all of a sudden going to church, being passionate about God, and Mum and Dad didn't seem to get it. We had endless arguments where I would tell them about my experience of God and how I believed he'd changed my life and they would tell me it was a load of rubbish and that I was taking it too far.

By this point we had been having 'differences of opinion' for approximately two years, so, as you can imagine, it was wearing thin. I will hold my hands up and admit that sometimes I did go a little too far. Sometimes it became a case of me preaching a sermon at them rather than discussing it in a mature and well-thought-out way. I ended up offending them, they ended up offending me and we pretty much followed that pattern for a while.

Don't get me wrong, my parents haven't always agreed with my decisions or my ways of doing things but they've always been there and supported me. Like when I decided to get baptised at the age of 16. Mum and Dad couldn't understand why I had to get baptised (full emersion baptism) as I'd already been christened as a baby and confirmed when I was 12. I said that when I'd been christened and confirmed I wasn't really making my own decision and being a Christian didn't mean to me then what it meant to me now. Mum and Dad didn't agree with or understand my decision but they supported me and came to my church to see me get baptised. However, none of that made it any easier to tell my mum and dad about leaving college!

The other thing was that I was doing really well in the subjects I had taken. I was on track for high grades and I'd got high grades in the GCSEs that I'd taken at the end of high school. Phrases such as, 'The world's your oyster' and 'You can be anything you want to be if you put your mind to it' were frequently used. This was going to be a lot harder than I thought.

It was about 10 o'clock at night. I'd been out and had been dropped off by one of my friends. I got out of the car and looked up at the house and noticed that Mum and Dad's bedroom light was on. I walked up the drive-way, put my key into the front door, walked in and softly closed the door behind me. All of the doors downstairs were shut, so I walked straight upstairs and went into Mum and Dad's bedroom to tell them I was home. The usual twenty questions were asked: 'Are you all right?' 'Have you had a nice time?' 'What've you been up to?' etc.

As they were asking me about my evening out, I tried to gauge what sort of mood they were in. Was this a good time to tell them my news? I quickly decided that if I didn't tell them now, I was never going to tell them . . . after all, there's no time like the present!

I sat on the end of the bed in a purposeful fashion and said, 'I've got something to tell you.' Time seemed to start running in slow motion as the books they were reading slowly reached their laps. They sat up a bit, slightly re-arranged the duvet and looked at me with eyes that said, 'Right . . . we're ready to listen.' Was I really going to do this? Was I really going to tell my parents that I was leaving college?

I remember hearing the words as they stumbled out of my mouth . . . 'I'm leaving college.' There . . . I'd said it. No turning back now.

Mum and Dad looked at each other in a confused manner and then came the one-word question that everyone hates to hear . . . 'Why?'

Before I could think of how to put it I said, 'Because God's told me to.'

NNNOOOOO! What had I just said?! That was the worst answer I could have given. I don't think anyone has ever answered a question so badly in the entire history of the universe. Please, ground, swallow me up! I'd really done it now.

I could see my mum's nostrils flaring as they always did when she was getting angry. She looked at me in an 'I'm really trying to be calm' way and said, 'Pardon?'

To my utter amazement the exact same words came out of my mouth once again, 'Because God's told me to.' This time I had a little squint in my eyes as I expec-tantly waited for my mum's internal fireworks to explode. For the next minute or so all I heard was Mum and Dad trying to be calm. But the more they talked, the louder and more high-pitched their voices became until they asked me another excruciating question.

'Well, what are you going to do when you've left college?'

Surely things couldn't get any worse than they were, so I said honestly, 'I don't know . . . God's told me to leave college and then he'll tell me what to do next.'

This time that really was 'it'! The internal fireworks went off all at the same time. Mum threw the bed covers off, got out of bed and began to stomp around the room. I think I actually closed my ears at this point because what was being said was not coming out as a pleasant noise! All I remember from that moment was how I remained adamant that I was going to leave college because God had told me to and how it was the final straw for Mum and Dad. They now thought that I really did belong in a loony bin and that, in the words of my mother, 'I was puddled.' After a while, we all knew that we weren't going to get any further and I went off to bed.

For the next few days things were pretty awkward but I remained confident that I'd done the right thing. I went into college and told my teachers that I wasn't going to be completing my A-level courses next year and that I would be leaving at the end of May 2002. When they asked that dreaded one-word question, I replied in the same way that I'd replied to my parents: 'Because God has told me to.' As you can imagine, that didn't do me any favours and they all thought it was a joke. Nevertheless, I knew what I had to do and I trusted that God knew what he was doing . . . or at least I sincerely hoped he knew what he was doing!

CHAPTER 10

LIFE-CHANGING STUFF

> " TAKE DELIGHT IN THE LORD
> AND HE WILL GIVE YOU
> THE DESIRES OF YOUR HEART "
> (Psalm 37v4)

A couple of weeks went by and I felt as if the world had been lifted off my shoulders. I'd made my decision and there was no going back on it now. I was praying like I'd never prayed before and asking God to take control of the situation that I found myself in.

Quite some time before all of this, on the day I got baptised, a lady called Debbie (Jon's mum, who used to drive the brown Volvo) bought me a book and wrote a Bible verse in the front of it. It was a verse from the Psalms and it said, 'Take delight in the Lord and he will give you your heart's desires' (Psalm 37:4). I held on to that verse so tightly in my heart and prayed that God would indeed give me my heart's desires. I knew that he had a plan and a purpose for my life; I knew that he wanted me to be a healer of broken hearts and I knew that I was going to use music as a way of doing that. All I wanted was to use the gifts that God had given me in the way that he wanted me to use them.

I kept swaying to and fro, to and fro. Had I made the right decision? Was this too big a risk to take? Why wasn't God now telling me what I was going to do next? It was as if he'd gone silent on me. I felt so isolated and so alone. My family didn't understand me, my teachers thought I was loopy, and all I wanted was to know that I'd made the right choice and that everything was going to work out OK. Why did all of this have to happen? I was perfectly happy with my life. I had my own plans and I knew what I wanted to do. I even had back-up plans. If I didn't make it as a singer, I wanted to be a journalist or work behind the scenes in some sort of media project. I was going to get married, live in a city somewhere and have children.

I had my life sorted and now it seemed like everything was falling apart at the seams.

Those two weeks or so were so difficult. I had to stay strong on the outside whilst on the inside I was consumed by doubt. And the worst part was that everyone was saying things like, 'Hasn't God told you what you're going to do yet then?'

I replied saying, 'No . . . but he will,' through gritted teeth.

It was a Monday evening – Monday, 25 February 2002, to be precise. I'd been to college, got home, had my tea and sat down at the computer. I thought I'd check my emails while I had a bit of spare time. I logged on to my email account and waited for it to load up. Most of my emails were junk mail but I noticed one that said 'audition this Friday'. I was intrigued. I clicked on it to open the email and this is what it said:

Hi Shell

My name is Chip Kendall. I work with an organisation called Innervation Trust, run by Mark Pennells and Zarc Porter (the guys who started The Tribe, V*enna and Shine). We were given the demo CD you sent to Alliance Music and we like what we've heard very much!

At the moment Innervation is looking for young talented people just like you to join us in a vision to see loads of young people presented with the good news of Jesus through the use of culturally relevant music, dance and live performance.

Basically, we're holding an important audition this Friday afternoon in Poynton (south Manchester) and we were wondering if you would be interested in coming. Obviously we realise this is extremely late notice but your CD has only just today come to our attention. So we'd appreciate it if you could come.

I've attempted to ring your mobile but it seems to be switched off whenever I try. I'll continue to keep trying but in case you get this message before I call, please feel free to call me at the Innervation office, or reply to this address.

Cheers! Hope to talk to you soon . . .

Chip

I screamed and immediately called my mum into the lounge where I sat staring at the computer screen. Mum rushed into the room and said, 'What? What?'

'Read this,' I said.

Mum read the email and her jaw practically hit the floor. She was completely shocked.

'Are you free to drive me to Poynton on Friday afternoon, Mum?' I asked excitedly, hoping and praying the answer would be 'Yes'. I was learning to drive at the time but hadn't passed my test, so the only other way of me getting there was by train. I didn't really want to have to go by train, though, because I wasn't very confident when it came to public transport. Mum checked her diary and it just so happened that she had booked Friday 1

March off work ages ago because she was owed a day off. I looked at Mum and said something that I'd been saying in my heart for the last five minutes but wasn't sure whether it was appropriate to say out loud. Oh . . . well . . . 'I knew God would pull through. I knew he'd do it!' I got off my chair and began jumping and skipping around the house.

Dad came home from work and I told him about the email. My dad isn't the most enthusiastic person in the world but you could tell that he, too, was astounded by what had happened.

That week was the longest week ever. I spent most of the time thanking God for giving me such a wonderful opportunity. My faith rocketed and every time I thought about the audition my heart would beat so fast. What song was I going to sing? What was I going to wear? How would I have my hair? After all, this audition could potentially change the rest of my life!

I arrived in Poynton at a church on the main village street where the auditions were being held. I'd never done anything like this before so I didn't have a clue what to expect and I felt sick with nerves. My mum parked the car and we walked into Poynton Baptist Church together. I had decided to have my hair down and I was wearing black trousers and a plain, cream jumper. Chip was there and so he introduced himself to me and told me to go and sit with the rest of the people who were auditioning. Mum went back to the car and sat and read her book.

Everyone was really friendly and I got chatting to a few of the other girls who were auditioning . . . still feeling very sick and shaking inside. Then, in through the doors walked a man wearing jeans and a black leather jacket, carrying a big 'boom box' style stereo system. It turned out to be Mark Pennells and, all of a sudden, I felt very intimidated. We were all told to come into the middle of the room because Chip was going to teach us a dance routine. I'd never done anything like this and wasn't really expecting it but I knew I had to give it my best shot. He taught us the routine so quickly and I really struggled to keep up. I hadn't danced for a couple of years because I'd torn my hamstring four times and had to give up my weekly dance classes when I was 15. But I got through it. Then we were split into groups and we had to perform it. There were people in that room who were far better dancers than I was but I didn't let that distract me too much. I made a few mistakes but I performed it to the best of my ability.

After we had all performed we were told that out of the fourteen or so of us that were there, five of us were going to be asked to stay and sing; the rest were going to be sent home. Mark was sitting at a table in a different room and each one of us had to walk over to him and face the decision. It was like something from *Pop Idol* or *The X Factor* and I had never been so nervous in my life!

Eventually it was my turn to go and hear the verdict. I forget word for word what was said but he said something along the lines of, 'Some of these people have auditioned before and it worries me that we've only seen you once. You're also really young.' My heart sank and I thought at that point that he was going to send me home. But then I heard him say, 'However . . . we would like you to stay so that we can hear you sing.'

I didn't know what to do with myself. I just smiled, said thank you and walked calmly back to my seat, whilst inside I just wanted to burst with excitement.

Five girls remained and they were all better dancers than me. I knew I had to impress Mark and Chip with my voice. Mark asked who wanted to go first and we all giggled and looked a little sheepish. I thought, *right* and put my hand up to go first. I stood in front of Mark, Chip and the other four girls, collected myself together and sang 'Can't Fight the Moonlight' by LeAnn Rimes. Mark looked at Chip with a hint of surprise on his face. They politely clapped and I sat down. The other girls sang and then it was time to go home.

That night Tim took me out for a pizza to celebrate. I hadn't been offered the job yet and was told that I would find out in the next week or so, but there was still reason to have a celebratory pizza!

Tim and I weren't an item at this point but we were still really good friends and I really believed we were destined to be together. I talked with such excitement about the audition and told Tim all about it. It turned out that I was auditioning to be in a schools band that Innervation Trust were setting up in Liverpool or Watford. Either way it would mean leaving home. Tim had realised that he didn't want me to go away and I think, between you and me, that he liked me more than he first thought! He said that he hoped I went to Liverpool rather than Watford because at least Liverpool was only half an hour away. I was touched by his thoughtfulness and realised that I didn't have to worry about our relationship because God had it under control.

A few weeks later I found out that I had got the job. I was amazed. Out of all the people who had auditioned I was the only one who had been offered the job! Let me explain to you exactly what it was going to entail . . .

Innervation Trust is a Christian charity that was set up by Mark Pennells and Zarc Porter. There were two parts to the vision. Firstly, they had a touring band called the-bandwithnoname who toured all over the UK doing concerts and festivals and using their music as a way of telling people about God. Secondly, they wanted to build up a network of schools bands, called Collective, that were dedicated to specific counties in the UK. I had auditioned to be in the first schools band that was going to be based in Liverpool (which Tim was very happy about!). The Collective bands would concentrate on working in the high schools of their designated county (in this instance Merseyside) using music and dance as a tool to tell young people about God. It was a full-time job but it was a voluntary contract. In other words, no one who worked for Innervation got paid.

This was the next hurdle that I had to jump over when it came to my parents approving of me doing this job. They didn't like the fact that I was leaving college to do something that I wasn't going to get paid for. I explained to them that we were going to be trained in how to raise our own sponsorship from people and organisations. Innervation Trust may not be paying me but I was going to get some money from somewhere. Despite my best efforts they just couldn't seem to get their heads round it. But, as always, I remained adamant that this was something I believed God was telling me to do and that nothing anyone said was going to stop me. (Do you remember me talking, earlier on, about that stubborn streak I had? Well, here it was in action!)

CHAPTER 11

A BIG SURPRISE

Defining moments in life are ones where we square up to fear, look straight into the face of pain, stand on God's wisdom and take hold of the plan that He has for our lives with confidence and strength. It is these moments that most people will run from. Those who have the courage to stand and be counted become history makers. Remember...
THE BATTLE IS NOT YOURS!

Changing the subject a little bit, I want to jump over to my relationship with Tim. Let me fill you in on a few of the details.

We'd originally started going out in December 2001. I had liked Tim for a long time before that but Tim, being the 'Mr Commitment freak' that he was, had played very hard to get! Eventually, my compelling personality and sheer beauty (hee hee hee . . . yeah, right!) got the better of him.

Now let me bore you with a little story that may tell you something about Tim and the way he was. That Christmas, Tim was going on a skiing holiday with three of his friends. I'm a very romantic person and thought I'd do something a bit special so that he would remember me whilst he was away. I bought a packet of Love Hearts sweets and some card, and cut the card up into rectangular pieces so that there was one for every day he was away. I then put a Love Hearts sweet on the left hand side of the card, wrote a little message on the right hand side and then covered it in sticky-back plastic. I did this several times, put them in separate envelopes and marked on the front the day he should open it.

I gave them to Tim as he was packing his suitcase and he put them in with the rest of his stuff. I thought it would be a lovely little keepsake and a way of helping him not to miss me too much. After all, if someone did that for me I would be so grateful. I'd open an envelope every morning with such pride and feel a little flutter in my tummy as I realised someone really did love me. But oh no . . . not Tim! Tim thought that the Love Hearts were there to be eaten!

When he got home from his trip, I was helping him to unpack his suitcase when I came across the demolished cards. The messages were unreadable, the plastic had been broken into, and the Love Hearts were gone! I looked at Tim and said, 'What's this?' Tim being Tim thought that I'd given them to him for consumption purposes, not as romantic keepsakes. He then went on to tell me how difficult it was to remove the Love Hearts sweets from the card because of the sticky-back plastic. I sat there with a look of horror on my face and tried to calmly explain to him that they hadn't really been designed for him to eat. They were simply little tokens of love! He began to look sheepish and replied by saying, 'Oh. Sorry babe, I didn't realise!'

Tim and I went out for a few months and then he decided to dump me a week before Valentine's Day. I was heartbroken . . . but, after a few days of crying into my pillow and comforting myself by eating lots of chocolate, I found that I wasn't too worried about it because I knew God had everything under control. We then ended up getting back together on 1 June 2002 after I'd invited myself to Tim's university end of year ball! We'd got all dressed up – Tim was in his tuxedo and I was in a gorgeous black ball gown – and (in good old 'Tim' style) we ended up getting the 'Magic Bus' to the Palace Hotel in Manchester, where the posh party was being held. I was expecting to be wooed by a limo or at least a taxi but no, we got on a busy, communal, blue and yellow, double-decker bus! I asked Tim through gritted teeth why and he responded by saying, 'Why spend money on getting a taxi when you can travel on the "Magic Bus" for 40p?'

What had I let myself in for? I soon realised that Tim had his funny ways of doing things and I learnt to love him for them . . . or should I say, despite them!

So, back to the main story. Mum and Dad had been bewildered by my new life for quite some time now and weren't jumping for joy about the decisions I'd made over the last couple of years. However, they went along with it and supported me.

It was August 2002 and Innervation Trust were holding a special commissioning event in Liverpool for the new 'Collective Merseyside' schools band. I was in the band with another girl called Tina and we had a team leader called Johnny G. None of us knew each other but we were all really excited about the adventure ahead of us. Tim and my parents had come with me to the event and were sitting with a load of other people. We listened to various people talk about the vision of Innervation Trust, we were introduced to everyone as the first Collective schools band, and then thebandwithnoname performed later on in the evening. It was a great event and I could feel myself getting excited by what I was going to be doing.

The event finished that night and we got in the car to go home. When we got home I asked my parents if they'd enjoyed it. You could tell they were a bit puzzled by the whole thing. Then Mum piped up and said, 'Does everyone who works for Innervation do it voluntarily?'

'Yes,' I replied.

There was a pause. Mum broke the silence by saying, 'I just don't understand why all of those people who are so incredibly talented would do it for nothing? They could potentially earn so much money but instead they've chosen not to?'

The next day, Collective Merseyside and thebandwithnoname ventured over to Warrington and thebandwithnoname performed at my church (Hillcliffe Baptist Church). It was an opportunity for my friends and church family to see what I was going to be spending the next two years of my life doing, and for me to try and raise some more monthly funding. My parents were intrigued to see how thebandwithnoname would be received by Hillcliffe Baptist Church and so decided to come to church with me.

It was a great service and, afterwards, we all went back to my mum and dad's house for some lunch. The guys were chatting to my parents about God for some time and they were having some pretty deep conversations, but you'll never in a million years guess what happened next . . . my mum and dad (the ones who had previously been against the whole 'church and God' thing) decided that they were going to do an Alpha Course! Once again I was totally speechless. I think the word to use in this situation is flabbergasted! Someone I knew from Warrington had invited my parents to take part in this Alpha Course and they had said 'yes'! Oh my goodness! I couldn't believe it! All this time they had been so opposed to it all and now, all of a sudden, they were interested in knowing more.

The Alpha Course is a ten-week course that provides an opportunity for people to explore Christianity in a relaxed and non-pressurised environment. You can ask questions about pretty much anything and listen to other people talk about their personal experiences of God. (For more info visit www.alpha.org) Were my parents really going to do an Alpha course?

A number of things were happening to my parents during that time. They'd been asking lots of questions about my faith – my mum had even been listening to thebandwithnoname's CD. I'd woken up and gone into Mum and Dad's room to find Mum sitting up in bed listening to her Walkman.

'What are you listening to?' I remember asking her.

'thebandwithnoname CD,' she blubbered.

I was very surprised by her answer for a number of reasons. One, she was listening to Christian music. Two, it was a combination of rock, hip-hop, rap and punk music – not really a style she was familiar with shall we say. And three, despite all of this, she was crying! Tears were actually streaming down her face. I leaned over to comfort her and asked her what was the matter.

'The words are amazing,' she said as more tears rolled down her cheeks.

I was speechless. My mum was crying at 'Take up the Tempo' by thebandwithnoname! As well as all of that, both my mum and my dad had had Holy Spirit moments. It was almost unbelievable.

Anyway . . . to cut a very long story short, over those ten weeks my mum and dad's hearts were transformed. They realised that Christianity wasn't about being part of a strict religion . . . it was about having a personal relationship with God. It was about experiencing God in a real way and realising that he wasn't out to get you, he just wanted to love you and for you to love him back. They became regular churchgoers at Hillcliffe Baptist Church and made lots of new friends. And then – the biggest decision of all – they got baptised together. Thebandwithnoname came to watch them make their public declaration of faith. I remember being there too and having to pinch myself to believe that it was really happening. It was an incredible moment and I thank God so much for the privilege of seeing that happen.

Dad is now a deacon at the church and my mum . . . well . . . talk about a little evangelist. They have led Alpha Courses in their church and seen God transform people just as he transformed them. They run weekly house groups and have worked on youth buses in the town. My dad even started a Christian union at his work. If ever I doubt that God has the power to transform people who I struggle to believe are transformable, I take one look at my parents and realise that anything is possible with God.

One of the most humbling moments of my life so far was when my mum said these words to me, 'Michelle, I'm so sorry for trying to stop you from doing what God wanted you to do and I'm so glad you didn't listen to me.' It just goes to show that God really can make the impossible possible!

CHAPTER 12

WHERE IT ALL BEGAN

LIVERPOOL

"When I heard that Shine and V*enna were disbanding I was completely gutted.

But now I am rejoicing on the roof tops because of this new schools team.

Way to go Innervation!"

Dave Sharples

'This is the most exciting thing to happen in Liverpool's schools since the abolition of corporal punishment. I am fully convinced that God is going to use this schools team to bring hundreds of young people to know Christ as their personal Saviour.'

Dave 'Captain' Sharples

I moved to Stockport, Greater Manchester in September 2002 to begin my training with Innervation Trust. I lived with Chip and his wife, Helen, and learnt a whole host of things about youth work and performing. We did a training course in evangelism called 'Xcellerate', we learnt how to communicate effectively, answer challenging questions, fundraise, etc. We learnt songs and dance routines and put a whole show together . . . all in the space of three months. We were worked hard but it was amazing!

Then, in January 2003, the hard work really did begin and I moved to Wavertree in Liverpool to start our work in the high schools of Merseyside.

It took us a while to get known amongst the high schools in Liverpool but once we were in it was amazing! I remember one of our very first schools weeks. We walked across the concrete playground over to the mobile classroom where we were going to be based and had stones thrown at us by some of the students. I remember thinking at that moment, *This is going to be more challenging than I thought!*

A typical schools week would include the following: approximately 15–20 1-hour lessons/workshops a week (these would be creative RE lessons, music lessons and/or dance lessons), assemblies, lunchtime concerts and then a big, 'end of the week' concert on the Friday night. We would transform the school hall by setting up a PA system, lighting rig and smoke machine and we'd put on a quality, high-energy show. It was at this concert that the young people would have an opportunity to decide whether or not they wanted God to be involved in their lives. Some of them said 'Yes' and genuinely wanted to have a personal relationship with God; some of them declined and simply got on with their lives. However, none of the young people ever stayed the same. They always finished the week knowing more about the Christian message and having been told about God's unconditional love for them.

We did the same thing in many high schools across Merseyside and got to see over 25,000 young people in the eighteen months we were there. What a privilege! Over 25,000 young people got to hear about God and his love for them and we witnessed some of the most incredible things.

I'll never forget one particular schools week during my time in Liverpool. We had a free lesson and I was on my way to get something out of the van. As I was walking over to the car park, I noticed a girl sitting on the floor with her back against a brick wall. She looked as though she'd been crying.

I went over to her and crouched down by her side. I looked at her face and then noticed a heap of tablets on the floor. 'Are you OK, sweetheart?' I asked.

The girl knew who I was because she'd been in one of our lessons earlier on in the week. She started to cry and told me that she wanted to kill herself. She was going to take a load of paracetamol tablets and wait to see what happened. If she'd taken all of them consecutively it would have caused serious damage, if not killed her.

I managed to get to the tablets and moved them out of her reach. She told me that she was getting bullied at school and that she felt worthless and insignificant. She couldn't cope with it any more and didn't see the point of living. I told her about the fact that God loved her more than she could imagine and that he hated seeing her so upset.

Eventually, I managed to persuade her to walk with me back into school. I sat her down in the reception area and got a member of staff to come and sit with us as I explained what was going on. From then on, the school took control of the situation and I had to write a statement about what had happened. I was just so grateful to God that I had been walking to the van at that time. If it had been a few minutes later, goodness knows what might have happened.

At the end of the week, the same girl came to our concert and decided to say 'Yes' to having a personal relationship with God. I had the privilege of praying with her and I asked God to help her realise how much he loved her. When we'd finished praying she gave me a hug and said, 'Thank you.' I still believe to this day that God had a plan in that situation. He directed my steps and put me in the right place at the right time so that I could assist the girl in her time of need and stop her from making a terrible mistake.

There were quite a few single sex schools in Liverpool and I remember the first all-girls school we went into. It was a Catholic school with a small chapel in the school grounds. We'd been given the chapel as our staff room where we could grab a cup of tea and have a few minutes' rest. As part of our creative RE lesson, I would always talk about my experience of having an eating disorder and how I believed God had transformed my life and healed me. My story always stirred up discussions about image and self-esteem. In this particular school we decided to invite the girls to come to the chapel during their break time to chat to us about any personal issues or struggles. Tina and I went to the toilet after our lesson and then headed back to the chapel.

To our astonishment we were greeted by a queue of approximately thirty girls. Tina and I sat down and called them in one by one. Each one of them came out with phrases such as, 'I feel fat', 'I'm ugly', 'I feel totally worthless', 'No one is ever going to love me', 'I'm on a diet but it's not working' etc. It was heartbreaking. Every one of the girls who entered that little chapel had such a low opinion of themselves and really disliked the girl they saw when they looked in the mirror.

I lived in a seven-bedroom house in Liverpool with the lovely Birch family. My room was situated on the very top floor. It was painted lime green, blue and yellow and filled with stuff that made it homely and comfortable. I had photographs up everywhere of all the people I loved. I had a single bed, a wardrobe, bookshelves, drawers, my computer and my keyboard. That night I went home, lay on my bed and burst into tears. I was so angry that there were so many girls who had such low self-esteem. I remember shouting at God and making my feelings very clear to him. Why had this affected me so much?

Was it because I'd been there, done that and worn the t-shirt and hated the thought of other girls going through similar things? All I knew was that I didn't like it and I wanted to be able to do something about it. I began to pray and ask God whether there was anything I could do to help these girls who struggled with self-image. As clear as anything I heard God say to me, 'Write a book.'

Write a book? How was an 18-year-old girl with very few qualifications going to write a book? I couldn't write a book! That was the most ridiculous thing I'd ever heard in my life. But then I stopped crying and thought, *Hang on a minute. Who says I couldn't write a book? I could write a book if I wanted to.*

I quickly sat up and thought about what to do next. I walked over to my computer, switched it on, pulled out the chair that was hiding under the desk and sat down. My legs were twitching and my heart was jumping as I waited for the computer to load up. I created a new Word document and stared at an empty page. What did I start with? Where did I begin? I remember writing the first few sentences and feeling as though my fingers were typing away without me even having to think about it. It was as if my hands weren't really attached to my body and they were just working by themselves.

That became a daily activity. I would spend every evening at my computer, typing away. I would read through my diary and write about some of the journeys that God had taken me on. I would read through the letters I'd written to Tim early on in our relationship and wait for ideas to spark. I wrote about times when I had experienced a lack of self-esteem and how I'd got through it. I wrote about how God had helped me to realise how much he loved me. I opened myself up and wrote about the good times, the bad times, my feelings, my thoughts and my emotions and I expressed my opinions on certain things. After three months, to my amazement, I had pages and pages of writing and all I had to do now was turn it into a book.

As you're probably beginning to realise, I'm not the sort of person who sits around waiting for things to happen – I'm proactive and like to get the ball rolling. So I decided to send my book to a couple of Christian book publishing companies. I wrote a covering letter explaining who I was and what the book was about and I sent it to Authentic Media and Scripture Union. I was very careful not to put my age on the covering letter because I was worried that people would see that it was written by an 18-year-old girl and wouldn't bother reading it.

I can't really remember how long it took to get a reply from the two companies but I do remember that my first reply was from Authentic Media. They wrote a letter to me saying that they weren't in a position to publish my book at this point and felt it needed too much work. Of course I was disappointed but not all hope was lost just yet – I was still waiting for a response from Scripture Union. And I will never forget the day that I got it. Scripture Union said that the book did need quite a bit of work but they were prepared to work on it with me because they felt it was something they would like to publish. I could not believe it – Scripture Union wanted to publish my book!

Just before she put the phone down on that initial phone call the lady asked me, 'Do you mind me asking you how old you are, Shell?'

'I'm 18,' I replied.

There was a brief pause before the lady said, 'Are you really? Well I never!'

It was pretty obvious that she was shocked and a little taken aback.

'That's not a problem is it?' I asked hesitantly.

'Not at all,' the lady replied. 'I just thought from your writing that you were a lot older than that but we are really excited about working with you, Shell.'

I later found out that Scripture Union had been sent over 300 manuscripts at that time and my book was one of two that were chosen to be published. I think it's safe to say that I was quite excited about the whole thing and I was incredibly grateful to God. I couldn't understand why God had chosen to use me after everything that had happened but I was so happy that he had!

CHAPTER 13

THE NEXT STEP

The next year flew by. Tim and I were still going strong and our relationship was growing each day. We'd gone through some very tough stuff at the beginning of our relationship which really tested us both but, as with most situations like that, it either tears you apart or makes you stronger and the latter was true for me and Tim. We were best friends above anything else. He knew everything about me and I knew everything about him – the good, the bad and the downright ugly!

We only really saw each other at weekends, because Tim was living in Warrington and was experiencing the dreaded 'first year of teaching' and I was living 20 miles away in Liverpool, still part of the schools band. We both had very busy lives but we made each other a priority and it worked.

Looking back, I don't know how we did it. I remember arriving back in Liverpool on a Sunday evening, going up to my room and crying because I felt so alone. Here I was, an 18-year-old girl in Liverpool, with all my family, friends and boyfriend back in Warrington. It sucked but I had to keep focused on why I was in Liverpool – to be a healer of broken hearts and to tell young people about God and his unconditional love for them. Keeping tight hold of the calling that God had placed on my life was what got me through my time in Liverpool.

When I first started the schools band, I knew it was only going to be for a season. I didn't really want to be doing this in ten years' time. I had signed a contract with Innervation Trust and had committed to being in the schools band for two years but I couldn't see myself being in it for longer than that. Don't get me wrong . . . I loved my job but it was hard work and, at times, it was a little tedious. We did the same lessons and performed the same songs week in, week out, and it became a chore to show constant enthusiasm. Working so closely with two other people had its ups and downs and the ridiculously early mornings were not fun. I am definitely not a morning person, so having to be out of bed at 5.30 a.m. and in school for 7.30 a.m. was disastrous for me. And then, to top it all off, we had to transport and set up our own sound system.

I remember a particular day in school when Mark Pennells (one of the directors of Innervation Trust and our boss) had announced he was coming over to Liverpool to break some news to us. Me, Tina and Johnny G wondered what it could be. For some reason we all used to get really uptight when Mark was coming over to see us. He somehow carried this authoritative and slightly intimidating demeanour about him. Not in a bad way, just in a 'let's get down to business' way. Mark was, and still is, someone who simply knows what he wants and makes it happen, and I admire him for that.

He walked in during one of our lessons wearing, as always, jeans, a shirt and his black leather jacket. He sat at the back of the classroom and watched us perform and present the lesson. At the end of the lesson he would always give us pointers and things to work on but he was generally pleased with what we were doing . . . I think!

The four of us went over to the dining hall and sat down at one of the long dining tables. The lunchtime bell hadn't gone yet and so the hall was empty apart from the odd lunchtime assistant walking through.

Mark began to tell us that the leadership team had decided to set up another touring band, like the the-bandwithnoname, but this touring band was going to be a pop band. As he told us more about this new project my heart began to sink. I so wanted to be in a touring band. I was enjoying my time in Liverpool but I'd started to feel as though I'd had enough. However, the more Mark told us about it the more apparent it became that neither Tina nor myself were going to be part of it. He'd just told us about it so that we knew what was going on and didn't hear about it from anyone else.

I remember feeling really deflated and generally gutted. Mark went on to tell us that we needed to keep doing what we were doing in Liverpool. He tried to encourage us that our work was of great importance and that it was making a difference, but nothing seemed to work. Tina and I were really disappointed that we were going to be stuck in Liverpool doing the same old same old, whilst this new and exciting project was going to be happening in Manchester at the Innervation head office.

Mark headed off back to Manchester and we continued with our day in school. None of us took the news that well and we spent a good chunk of the afternoon having a moan about it. But, somehow, I had a real peace about it all and sensed that God knew exactly what he was doing and was in control. I knew I didn't have to worry about it – I just needed to get on with what I was doing and focus on doing it well.

A few months passed and, don't hold me to it, but I think it was around the November of 2003 when Johnny G suddenly got a phone call one morning from Mark asking us all to go over to the Innervation head office in Manchester. Mark had a meeting with each of us, one at a time – Johnny G, then me and then Tina. I remember sitting there wondering what was so important that he had to tell us all separately.

The Innervation office at that time was in a three-storey house that was located at the bottom of a quiet cul-de-sac in Stockport, Greater Manchester. On the ground floor there was the entrance hall and Zarc's recording studio; on the first floor there was a lounge that was converted into a communal office space, a kitchen and a bathroom; on the second floor was Mark's office (that we sometimes used as a rehearsal room) and two other rooms that were mainly used for storage.

I walked up the stairs and into Mark's office. I sat down and nervously waited to hear what Mark had to say. Mark started to talk about the new touring band and all I can remember is that feeling of disappointment re-visiting me as I listened to him talk.

Suddenly I heard him say, 'Shell, we'd like you to be in the new touring band.' That feeling of disappointment was very quickly replaced by a state of shock and I found myself not really knowing what to say. I remember thinking all sorts . . . *What about the schools band? What about Tina and Johnny G? Where will I live? Am I good enough to be in a touring band?* . . . endless questions circling in my mind.

The plan was for me to continue in the schools band in Liverpool until June 2004, but also be in the touring band at the same time. Then, from July 2004, I would be in the touring band full time. There were a few little issues like the fact that they hadn't found anyone else to be in the new touring band yet and they didn't have a name for it, but aside from that this was all definitely happening and I was the happiest girl in the world!

Tina didn't take the news too well (if I were in her shoes at the time, I wouldn't have taken it too well either) and our friendship really suffered as a result of the decisions that had been made. But despite the repercussions I was still delighted that I'd been asked to be in a touring band. I remember getting in my 'sundance red' Peugeot 106 and driving home to tell Tim and my family the good news. I was beaming and drove the whole way home with a big fat smile on my face. I was praying and thanking God for this wonderful opportunity – thanking him for giving me a peace about it all when I was first told about the touring band a few months before. I remember sitting in the car and feeling as if being in a touring band was all I'd ever been designed to do and now it was finally happening!

Suddenly, as if from nowhere, I heard God say to me, 'To whom much is given much is required.' Everything within me came to a sudden halt (apart from the car!) and my smile vanished.

I questioned what I'd just heard and once again God said, 'Shell, to whom much is given, much is required.' Then everything within me started up again, my smile resurfaced and I said, 'OK God . . . that's cool.'

I didn't really understand what God meant at the time, so I just brushed it off with a quick reply. But let me tell you this – if I'd known then what I know now, I wouldn't have brushed it off so easily. You see God was warning me – protecting me if you like – about the dangers of responsibility. Spiderman is warned about the same thing: 'With great power comes great responsibility.' If you speak it quickly it doesn't seem to mean that much but if you take the time to think about what those words actually mean, it takes your breath away. God was moving me into a new season, a new chapter of my life. This new part of the journey required more from me in so many ways . . . if only I'd known just how much more.

CHAPTER 14

ANOTHER BIG SURPRISE

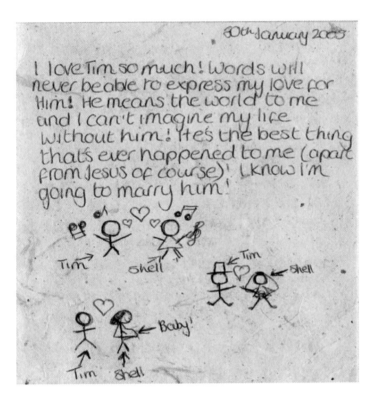

I'd decided, given the situation, to move back to Warrington and live with my parents. Warrington lies right in the middle of Manchester and Liverpool, so it would only take me thirty minutes to get to either place. The other bonus of living there was that I would get to see Tim more, and considering our relationship was better than it had ever been, that was a very good thing!

Life in the schools band was difficult because I was preparing myself to be in the touring band – but I felt unable to throw myself fully in to the touring band because I was still in the schools band. One week I would be rehearsing new dance routines and recording new tracks in the studio for the touring band and the next week I'd be back in Liverpool doing a schools week with songs and dance routines I'd been doing for the last eighteen months. On top of all that, I was still at this point working on my book and trying to get it as good as it could possibly be.

It was a stressful time of life but all I could do was get on with it and do my best. It was great to be back at home and Tim and I got to see each other so much more. I got to spend time with my friends again and my relationship with my parents and brother was amazing. Having the people I loved around me was what got me through that transition period . . . goodness knows what I would have done without them.

Before I knew it, it was April 2004. The touring band now had a name. It was to be called . . . drum roll please . . . 'tbc'. I'd recorded a single, the very first tbc song ever, called 'Mind Your Head' with a B-side track called 'Sorry and Safe' and we were just about to do our first load of gigs at one of the biggest Christian festivals in the UK – Spring Harvest. Now, I use the term 'we' very loosely because at this point, the only full time member of tbc was me. We'd desperately searched for other people to be in the band and had come close to finding people a few times but none of them had worked out. And so the first nine months of tbc was me along with various other combinations of girls that included Helen K, Tina, Liz, Laura, Nat, Naomi and Kyra. Eventually, in January 2005 (note that's over a year since I'd been asked to be part of tbc!), the official line up of tbc was announced . . . Liz, Laura, Nat and Shell . . . Let the fun begin!

But before I tell you about life on the road . . . I need to tell you about something even more significant that happened in my life. Let me take you back to April 2004. I was living in Stockport with the amazing Phillips family. I was living with them for a couple of weeks on a trial basis to see if I wanted to live with them (and they wanted me to live with them!) permanently from July 2004. I moved in with them for my two-week trial on the 30 or 31 March. There was Liz and Roger and their two crazy sons, Tim and Matthew. Matthew was the same age as me and Tim was a little bit older.

I had to be up quite early for work on the Thursday of that week and that Thursday turned out to be April Fool's Day. Nothing was mentioned in the house about it nearly being April Fool's Day and I slept soundly the night before thinking, *There's no way they'll play any tricks on me when I've only just moved in.*

I woke up early on the Thursday morning, put my dressing gown on and opened my bedroom door to go across the landing and in to the bathroom to have a wash. But there was a small problem. Two boys by the names of Tim and Matthew had decided to make this simple act difficult for me by taping thick, white paper across the frame of my door so that when I opened my bedroom door all I could see was a big smiley face and the words, 'April fool!'

Just for a minute try to put yourself in my shoes . . . It's early in the morning (and I'm not a morning person) . . . I'm waking up in a strange house with people I've known for a grand total of two days, if that . . . I'm worried about making my way to the bathroom in case I open the wrong door and end up in someone else's bedroom . . . but I can't even get out of my room because the whole door frame has been blocked with paper and sticky tape! As you can imagine I was slightly shocked. But instead of ripping the paper down, gathering it up, walking into Tim or Matthew's bedroom and shoving it in their face (which I would have done if I'd known them for more than two days), I was frightened of waking anyone else up. So I rooted around my room for some scissors and quietly cut my way through so that I could complete the unusually difficult task of making my way to the bathroom. All of that would have put some people off but it was from that moment that I knew I wanted to live there permanently!

So . . . back to the story. I was living in Stockport for a few weeks with the crazy Phillips family whilst we did the final rehearsals for tbc's debut performance at Spring Harvest '04. Days were mad busy and all I wanted to do during the evenings was chill out and relax. I love going out for big, slap-up dinners, being waited on hand and foot, and then going home without having to do any washing up – and who better to enjoy that experience with than the love of my life . . . Tim.

Tim was driving to Stockport to see me quite a bit because I was going to be away at Spring Harvest for two weeks. Normally, he would come over to my house and we would sit and watch the TV or go out for a walk, or sit and have a little cuddle, but this time it was different. In the space of a week we must have visited every restaurant in Bramhall village (a posh little village on the outskirts of Stockport). I remember it so well because I hated olives at the beginning of the week and by the end of the week I loved them! Tim kept telling me it was 'an acquired taste' and that the more I tried them the more I'd end up liking them and, as always, he was right! But there's another reason I remember that week so well . . .

It was the night before I was off to Spring Harvest and we went to the only restaurant in Bramhall that we hadn't yet visited – The Orange Tree. It was one of the more sophisticated places to eat in the village at the time, so we put on our glad rags and got our taste buds ready to enjoy a fabulous meal.

We started off with an 'Orange Tree special' – fresh bread, olive oil, balsamic vinegar and hummus. Then we had our 'melt in the mouth' main course, during which my mum called me to tell me that she'd managed to get tickets to see Cliff Richard and Donny Osmond (the two loves of her life) on the same weekend! She was obviously very excited about it but Tim got rid of her pretty quickly so as not to spoil the atmosphere. It was perfect – conversation was flowing, red wine was being poured, great food, great company . . . What more could a girl ask for?!

We finished our main course and Tim handed me a handwritten letter. We quite often wrote letters to each other and so I was really happy to be handed this folded piece of paper. I opened it and quietly read it. It became apparent that he'd written me a song and it went something like this . . .

Bridge: You said to me I was the one
Right from the start you seemed to know
And as I look into the future... you are there

(Last verse)
(Im D or F)

So now this song is over
And yet we've just begun
Through thick and thin I'll stick by you
I promise to take care
For now I know there is no other
to make my life complete
I'm down on one knee... and asking please......
marry me!

So Babe?

I looked up at Tim and said, 'Aww babe . . . that's lovely! Thank you so much.'

Tim looked a little surprised.

I put the letter down on the table and waited for conversation to start up again. Tim still looked shocked.

'Have you read that last bit properly?' he said.

I picked up the letter and re-read the last paragraph. I got to the last sentence and the words 'marry me' seemed to jump off the page right at me. I took a very loud and sharp breath in. I looked at Tim and he smiled at me. I couldn't get my head round what was happening.

Tim then rummaged around in his pocket and placed a small, burgundy box on the table and pushed it towards me. Was this really happening or was I dreaming? He told me to open the box . . . so I did. Inside was a beautiful 24-carat gold engagement ring with a big diamond in the middle and five little diamonds either side. I looked at the ring, looked at Tim and the biggest smile ever appeared on my face. Then Tim said, 'Well . . . will ya?'

In all the excitement I'd forgotten to say yes! I nodded my head vigorously and said, 'Of course I will!'

Tim took the ring out of the box, placed my left hand in his and pushed the ring onto my fourth finger. It was far too big because for some reason I have very small hands but it was perfect in every other way. I then started shrieking at the top of my voice, ran round to Tim and flung my arms around him. The whole restaurant knew at this point what was going on and that was fine by me because I wanted the whole world to know that the man of my dreams had just asked me to be his wife!

I went back to my seat and then proceeded to phone every person on my contacts list to tell them that Tim and I were officially engaged! Everyone was so pleased. We left the restaurant and went to the Trafford Centre to take my ring in for re-sizing. It wasn't going to be done straight away so I didn't have a ring for the first two weeks of being engaged, but that didn't matter. All that mattered was that I was soon to become Mrs Perris and spend the rest of my life with Tim.

We got back to the Phillips household and Liz and Roger had opened a bottle of bubbly to celebrate . . . the whole evening was just perfect. I think it's safe to say that 7 April 2004 was one of the best days of my life. Tim had made me the happiest girl in the world. All we needed to do now was plan our wedding!

The next day I went to Spring Harvest with Helen, Tina, Liz and Laura, and I went round telling everyone I knew about the news of our engagement. It was really hard being away from Tim and I later found out that he'd been having loads of parties to celebrate without me! Oh well, never mind!

Spring Harvest was great – it was extremely hard work but great! Everyone loved the new single and 'Mind Your Head' mania broke out in the 8–11s venue! We performed every day and every night and our schedule was a bit mental, but it was fab and I enjoyed every minute of it. After all, this was what I'd wanted for so long and now it was finally happening!

So much happened in the next year in terms of tbc and it was a year of preparation for me in every sense of the word. In terms of tbc we did loads of little gigs all over the country, each one with a different line-up! In the November of that year the official line up was decided (Liz, Laura, Nat and Shell) and we had so much to do: styling, photo shoots, interviews, rehearsals, etc. We recorded our debut, self-titled album and put a whole show together in a really short space of time.

Tim and I decided on a date for the wedding and started planning the big day. We'd decided to get married in the following February, so we had only ten months to get everything ready. We chose a venue, chose the menu, wrote a guest list, chose our best men (Tim had two best men because he couldn't decide who he wanted!), bridesmaids and ushers. I tried on endless wedding dresses and eventually found 'the one'! We picked the flowers, the cake, the favours, the colour schemes, the men's attire, the wedding cars, the invitations, and the bridesmaids' dresses. We booked the church and the photographer and the jazz band for the evening entertainment, the list of 'things to do' was endless. But before we did any of that we went house hunting.

We found a little house that we loved, close to the centre of Stockport. But then, three months before the wedding, the sellers pulled out and we were left with no house to move in to. So we viewed some more houses and found another house round the corner on Shaw Road South. We fell in love with it straight away, got the ball rolling and picked the keys up about three weeks before the wedding. It was all a bit stressful. We got all of our family round, slapped some magnolia paint on the walls so that it was a little more liveable and realised we had no money left to buy any furniture! But have no fear, God provided for us in unimaginable ways. We were bought a bed and a dining table; two of my mum's work colleagues were moving in together and had a house full of stuff they didn't need, so they invited us to go round and take anything we wanted! They ended up giving us a sofa, a washing machine, a fridge-freezer, kitchen utensils, shelves, wardrobes, everything! We were given a futon, a microwave, a TV, a stereo system . . . and all of this was before we'd even received any wedding gifts! I'd even been given some money when I moved to Liverpool to buy a kettle, a toaster, a pan set, a dinner set and some cutlery, so we already had all that as well. It was amazing and we would often stand in our house, look around and just thank God for his limitless provision.

February 2005 finally arrived. Tim and I were going to be tying the knot in twelve days' time and there was so much to be done. I'd been working really hard with tbc getting ready for our first tour that was going to be starting on 10 March. We'd been getting the house ready, packing our stuff up ready to move it all in to our new home, having our final dress/suit fittings, doing wedding rehearsals and marriage preparation classes, and packing for our honeymoon to New York, USA. Just over a week before the wedding, Tim lost his passport and had to rush a new one through the passport office so that it was ready in time, and my new passport in the name of Michelle Leanne Perris had arrived! It was all running very smoothly and everyone was beginning to get very excited!

The day before the wedding we got notification that the postman tried to deliver a parcel to our new house. We drove over to the sorting office in Stockport to pick it up. I thought it would be a wedding gift but it wasn't – it was the first copy I'd ever seen of my new book that was going to be out in the April after our wedding!.I opened it up and there it was . . . *In These Shoes?!* by Shell Perris. I couldn't believe it! My very first book in its finished form. All the hard work, all the sweat, all the tears that had gone into making the book . . . it was now all worth it. I had a tear in my eye as I flicked through it and thanked God for giving me such an incredible opportunity.

It got to 4 p.m. and Tim and I said goodbye, as I stayed at my mum and dad's house and Tim went for a drink with his best men. That night, I had my final night as Michelle Whittaker and spent it reminiscing with my parents. My friend Nikki came round to see me and give me some words of wisdom and advice, and I went to bed with butterflies in my tummy and anticipation for my wedding day! I wrote a little note to God, asking him to help me to be a good wife in this new chapter of my life, and then I turned off the light and managed to have a peaceful night's sleep.

CHAPTER 15

THE DAY WE SAID 'I DO'

THIS DAY
I WILL MARRY
MY BEST FRIEND;
THE ONE I LAUGH WITH,
LIVE FOR,
DREAM WITH,
LOVE...

Saturday, 12 February 2005 – my wedding day had finally arrived! The day I'd dreamt of since I was a little girl was here and I was going to enjoy every single minute of it.

I woke up and my mum brought me breakfast in bed. The postman knocked on the front door with some wedding cards and a parcel that turned out to be a set of crystal glasses from Authentic Media (Authentic were tbc's record label at the time). I tried to remain as calm as possible as I had a bath and began to get ready.

My bridesmaids arrived and the tbc girls were there, too, helping out and making sure everyone's hair and make-up was done. The photographers arrived and started to take pictures of us all as we got ready. Mum got dressed into her beautiful mother-of-the-bride outfit, Dad and Craig put their suits on, the bridesmaids put their dresses on and then it was time for me to put my dress on. I got dressed downstairs in the front room because I was frightened of walking downstairs in my wedding dress and falling over! The flowers were delivered and everything and everyone was ready to go.

Craig went to the church first because he was one of Tim's ushers. Then the wedding car arrived and Mum and the bridesmaids went to church to get ready. My dad and I closed the door and that was when the real butterflies started to flutter away deep in my belly!

The car came back. Dad and I walked down the driveway and got into the car. I looked at him and he looked at me and we both smiled as the car began to make its way to the church. We were getting married at Hillcliffe Baptist Church because it had played such a big part in our lives individually and together. We drove up the steep driveway to the church and pulled up outside the front entrance a few minutes before 1 p.m. My dad has never been late for anything in his life and he was not about to change that . . . especially not on his daughter's wedding day.

ORDER OF SERVICE

This day I will marry
my best friend;
the one I laugh with,
live for, dream with,
love . . .

MR. TIMOTHY JAMES PERRIS

and

MISS. MICHELLE LEANNE WHITTAKER

Saturday 12th February 2005
Hillcliffe Baptist Church

Minister:	Rev. Bill Eugster		
Best man:	Dan Curtis	**Ushers:**	Craig Whittaker
Best man:	Ric Murawski		Tim Dyson
			Andrew Perris
			Daz Percival

Bridesmaids: Emma Perris
Georgia Pennells
Ella Pennells

Worship Band: Doug Walker, Steve Biltawi, Don Harding, Jon Lucas

I remember it being a really cold and windy day but I didn't feel cold at all. My veil nearly blew off a couple of times but that was about it. Dad and I stood in front of the car and had some photos taken and then we made our way into the entrance hall of the church. Daz and Andy (two of Tim's ushers) were waiting for me and everything seemed to be in order. All I needed to do now was relax and enjoy the day.

The day we said 'I do' was one of the best days of my life so far. It was a milestone – the day when I became Mrs Timothy Perris. Life was not about 'me' any more; it was about 'us'. Two people joining together and becoming one. It was full of memories that I will treasure deep in my heart forever. I remember sitting at the top table during the reception and making a point of looking around to take in everything that was going on: people laughing, wine flowing, children playing, everyone simply relaxing and enjoying themselves. It was truly amazing and I loved every minute of it.

The next day we jetted off to New York City for our honeymoon and had a fabulous week. We got back to our new house to find that Tim's brother and his wife had decorated the front of the house with balloons and big 'welcome home' banners. Then we were faced with the mammoth task of opening our wedding gifts. And then, once all the glitz and glamour had been and gone, it was back to the real world where our marriage really began.

Looking back, the first month of me and Tim living together was hilarious. We had never lived together before and all of a sudden we found ourselves sharing everything . . . a house, a bed, a sofa, a TV. We were certainly made aware of each other's annoying little habits very quickly! Tim hated how I never finished a cup of tea. I hated how Tim never unbuttoned his shirts before he put them in the washing basket. We even argued about which way round to put the toilet roll on the toilet roll holder! We each had our own ways of doing things and we soon found that our individual ways didn't always match up. That first month was a time where we got to know each other in a completely different way and we were forced to learn the art of compromise! Despite all the ups and downs, it was great and I look back on that first month of marriage with very fond memories.

CHAPTER 16

LIFE ON THE ROAD

Live your life freely in His love, in the knowledge that there is nothing happening in life where He hasn't gone before you... and nothing happening that you and Him can't deal with together. Keep yourself open to Him and there is no telling how much God can achieve through you.

The second, third, fourth and fifth months were an entirely different story. On 10 March 2005, twenty-six days after we had tied the knot, tbc began a sixty-date tour. I knew that being in tbc and being married was going to be tough but nothing could have ever prepared me for what was about to happen.

Let me paint you a little picture. I'd been married for under four weeks and all I wanted was to be at home with my new husband. Four 20-year-old girls with big personalities all on the road together and living in each other's pockets, days of early mornings and late nights, performing, sweating, and sometimes even being sick because we were working so hard. Some may say it was a recipe for disaster and a part of me would tend to agree. However, even though we were away from Thursday to Sunday (sometimes Monday) every week for four months, and despite the fact that we sometimes argued and did each other's heads in, I look back and think 'Wow!' What an amazing opportunity. When I think about it logically, that tour changed my life. Not only did I learn so many things about myself and other people, it was when I became an evangelist.

Our first tour date was in Letchworth, UK and a couple of days before we'd had a dress rehearsal at a church in Cheadle Hulme, Stockport. When the dress rehearsal had finished, me, Liz, Laura, Natalie and Mark all sat down to make sure everything was sorted. We suddenly remembered that someone needed to do a talk at the end of the concert. Mark thought about it for a few minutes and said, 'Shell . . . you do it.' At first I panicked. I'd never preached before and I had only two days to prepare what I was going to say. All I could do was pray and trust that God would give me the words to say.

We arrived in Letchworth, unloaded the van, set up, soundchecked, had dinner, got changed and stood backstage ready to 'do our thing'. I remember feeling as if I was going to wet my pants, I was that nervous. Not only did I have to perform, I also had the task of preaching hanging over my head.

Before I knew it, we were on stage, singing our songs and dancing like there was no tomorrow. It was amazing! We always finished our concert with the song 'Loved', and then it was time for me to pick up my Bible and preach. I would not be able to tell you what I said that night if you asked me. I just remember feeling as though God was totally in control.

The whole point of doing a talk at the end of our concert was to tell people about Jesus and how much he loved them. It was also about giving people an opportunity to respond to what had been said by choosing whether or not they wanted to be a follower of Jesus.

I remember standing on stage and looking around the room at a couple of hundred faces that seemed to be listening intently. You could have heard a pin drop. I spoke about how God's love had transformed my life and about how it could transform their lives if they wanted it to. And then it got to the bit where they were invited to make a choice that could potentially change their lives. So many thoughts and emotions were racing through my mind. My palms were sweating, my hearting was pounding and I eventually plucked up the courage to ask the question that my whole talk had been steering towards: 'If any of you in this room would like to invite Jesus into your lives and allow his love to transform you, I would like you to stand up now.' There was silence.

I was standing there thinking, *God, please give these people the strength and courage to stand up and choose to live their lives for you . . . please . . . please . . . please* . . . And then, out of the corner of my eye, I saw someone stand up and a party started in the depths of my soul. *Thank you, God . . . thank you, God.* Then another person stood to their feet and the party in my soul continued. Then another person stood up . . . and another . . . and another . . . and then a few more . . . and then even more. After a few seconds, 75 per cent of the people in that room were standing and had made the decision to say, 'Yes, I want to be a follower of Jesus and I want him to make a difference in my life.' We were all speechless and couldn't believe what had just happened! In my heart, all I could say was, *Thank you, God . . . Thank you, God . . . Thank you.*

I have quite a few fond memories from that tour but the best one was when we performed at the smallest nightclub you have ever seen in Devon. It took us about six hours to drive down there and we pulled up in a little car park outside the venue. We unloaded our stuff and then went across to the local church hall to have some lunch.

We got talking to the event organisers and got on to the subject of home schooling. It turned out that they home-schooled their children so that the whole family could spend three months of the year in Kosovo. I, knowing very little about geography and having no idea where Kosovo was, stupidly said, 'Oooh Kosovo . . . all right for some!'

Everyone in the room looked at me as the lady said, 'Yeah, if dodging landmines and seeing people die is your idea of a holiday!'

I very quickly remembered that there'd been a pretty horrible war in Kosovo; these people were going out there on a mission trip to help those who had suffered as a result of the war. I couldn't believe what I'd just said and continued to eat my dinner until the long, uncomfortable silence passed.

That night I was preaching and I'd been told that most of the young people who were coming to the concert were un-churched. I very rarely remember what I say when I preach because God just seems to take over. But I remember what happened when I asked the question I always asked at the end of my talk: 'If anyone in this room would like to invite Jesus into their lives and allow his love to transform you, I would like you to stand up now.' Within a matter of seconds every single person in the entire room stood to their feet, about a hundred in total.

At this point I didn't do what I normally do – because I told them all to sit down again! I realise that the number one rule in the 'Evangelists Guide to Preaching' is probably 'Never tell people who have stood up during the response time to sit down again' but I thought I'd been misheard.

So everyone sat down. I then took a further five minutes saying, 'This isn't a joke, it's very serious. You should only stand up if you really want to. Don't do it because your friend is, and don't do it because you feel under pressure.' I even said, 'I'd rather a handful of people stood up and really mean it than all of you stand up and be messing around.'

I composed myself and asked the same question again . . . 'If anyone in this room would like to invite Jesus into their lives and allow his love to transform you, I would like you to stand up now.' Instantly everyone stood up. I was amazed!

In the space of four months we saw thousands of people say 'Yes' to Jesus. What a privilege to be used in that way and to see so many lives transformed. I remember doing my very first radio interview with Wayne Clark on BBC Radio Merseyside, just before I started working in Liverpool as part of Collective Merseyside. He asked me what my expectations were and why I was doing it all and my answer was this: 'If one person's life is changed and they say "Yes" to Jesus as a result of God working through me in some way, then I'll be happy.' It just goes to show that God can exceed and shatter expectations and he has the ability to do far more than we could possibly dream of or imagine. Maybe we should forget about human expectations and have the audacity to dream big, believing that God can do the impossible. After all, if there's one thing I've learnt over the years it's this: human expectations may prevent us from being disappointed but they limit God.

I was in tbc for just under three years and I can honestly say it was an amazing experience and an utter privilege. We released an album, a DVD, performed all over the UK and in parts of Europe, did mission weeks in primary schools, released a joint track with thebandwithnoname on itunes, did radio interviews, TV interviews . . . But most importantly we saw God transform thousands of lives and he used us all in ways beyond our imagination.

However, it was one of the hardest things I have ever done and, at times, I would have done anything to not be part of it. But that was partly due to my lack of experience and inability to deal with situations and people in the right way. I learnt an awful lot about myself during my time in tbc, most of which was pretty hard to deal with. It's not always easy to look in the mirror and see someone you never wanted to be staring back at you. In three years you can make some pretty bad choices and I think it's fair to say that I made my fair share. I am more than happy to hold my hands up and say that towards the end of my time in tbc I had become quite arrogant without realising it, and my true identity was beginning to get squashed by my 'super self'. That was when I knew it was time to leave.

CHAPTER 17

WE'VE ONLY JUST BEGUN

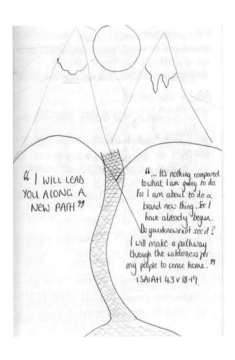

I spent the next five months chilling out and resting after a pretty hectic few years. I spent some much needed quality time with Tim and enjoyed being a stay-at-home wife. For the first time in our married life I had time to do the washing and cleaning, and I started to enjoy cooking proper meals instead of always having stuff that came straight out of the freezer. I spent time with family and friends, had pyjama days, went shopping and did all the things I hadn't had time to do for the last three years. It was fantastic! A couple of months after I'd left tbc, Tim and I made a last-minute decision to go camping. So we chucked our things in the car and headed off to France for a month and had the best holiday ever!

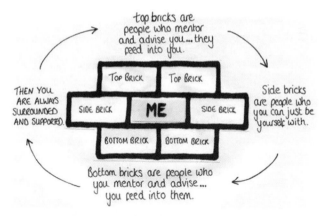

I was part of Innervation Trust for four and a half years in total and although I had the time of my life, I also came away with a lot of baggage that needed dealing with before I could move on to anything else. I needed to give God space and time to do what he needed to do within me, and that's where Trevlyn came in. Trevlyn is the wisest and most caring lady I have ever met in my life and she is what I would call my 'Top Brick'! Sounds a little strange, I know, but let me explain.

Trevlyn used her God-given gifts of listening, counselling and wisdom to guide me and advise me, and without her I wouldn't be the person I am today. I know she would say she didn't do that much but to me she did exactly what I needed. She allowed me to see God in a completely different light and get to know him in a deeper and more intimate way. During those five months my relationship with God was transformed. As a result I was healed, restored and I experienced God's grace. God dealt with me in such a gentle way and pointed out things in me that I didn't even know existed. He took me on a journey where I faced some of my fears, came to terms with some of my weaknesses and underwent some major Holy Spirit heart surgery. God does 'exactly what it says on the tin' when it comes to transformation.

So . . . what now? During my five months of rest I spent a lot of time thinking about what God had called me to be. I wrote loads of songs about some of the things I was going through at the time and re-visited songs I'd written in the past. Songwriting was something that I was really passionate about. I learnt a lot from Mark and Zarc whilst working for Innervation and I watched how they wrote songs. I knew that song writing was something I wanted to do. After all, God had called me to be a healer of broken hearts through *my* music. So I thought about it logically and asked myself this question: 'If I could do anything right now, what would it be?'

The answer seemed simple to me. I wanted to do what I've always wanted to do – be a singer/songwriter and heal broken hearts through my music. So that's what I set out to accomplish.

By this point I had a really good relationship with Authentic Media. They had been tbc's record label and they had published my second book, *Something to Shout About*, so it seemed natural for me to approach them first about my new venture. I phoned Dave Bruce who was the 'Music Man' (as I liked to call him!) at the time and arranged a meeting with him. I travelled down to Milton Keynes on 12 September 2006, had a meeting with Malcolm (the 'Book Man') about some book stuff and then stepped into Dave Bruce's office and took a seat.

Looking back I can't believe I was so bold! I remember sitting there and making polite conversation with Dave. My palms were sweating, my heart was racing and my cheeks shook a little with nerves as I smiled. And then after ten minutes or so of chitchat the serious talks began.

I started telling Dave about the calling that I believed God had placed on my life to be a healer of broken hearts through my music and a light to the nations. I told him about all the things that I sensed God had been say-ing to me and a little bit about the experiences I'd had so far. I then went straight in to talking about how I wanted to be a singer/songwriter and how I'd love to do my own album and embark upon a solo career. I 'just happened' to have a demo of a song that I'd written with a friend of mine called Dave Healey (my music teacher's husband who I'd recorded my demos with. He randomly got in touch at just the right time after losing contact), and Dave Bruce played it in his office. It was a song called 'Where is My Happy Ending?' Dave seemed very impressed and liked what he heard. We then went on to speak about what style of music I wanted to do and how I saw it happening, etc. And then, after an hour or so, Dave said, 'Yes, I think we can sort something out.' My jaw hit the floor, my eyes grew wide and a big fat smile appeared across my face. Here I was, a very nearly 22-year-old girl, sitting in Dave Bruce's office, asking if he would give me a record contract and he had pretty much just said yes. I could not believe it! Talk about God's favour and perfect timing. I felt incredibly blessed and so grateful. This was what I'd always wanted to do and I felt as if my dream was beginning to come true.

Over the next few weeks quite a few emails were exchanged, and the next thing we had to do was find someone to produce the songs. Quite a few people were considered, including Mark and Zarc, but in the end Simon Hill and Rob May from Sitting Duck Productions in Oxfordshire were employed to produce my songs. I went on their website to find out a bit more about them and was bowled over when I saw the list of people they had worked with/for in the past: Natasha Beddingfield, Victoria Beckham, Fame Academy, Westlife, S Club 7, Emma Bunton, Misteeq, Honeyz . . . the list went on! I was so excited and couldn't wait to start work in the studio. It was decided that I would do a five-track EP first to see how it went, which I was more than happy with, and on 16 January 2007 I signed my very first solo record contract!

That was the beginning of a brand new adventure for me, and one that I had dreamt of for a long time. I felt as though I was exactly where God wanted me to be. I'll never forget the wise words of Zarc. I'm not sure whether he came up with these words himself or whether someone else told him – either way, they are pretty profound . . .

> You always know when God is in the middle of something – an idea, a project, or a dream – because it feels as if you're travelling at a hundred miles an hour on a bicycle and when you look down at your feet, you realise you're not even pedalling. When God isn't in the middle of an idea, a project or a dream, you feel as if you're pedalling at a hundred miles an hour and then realise you're not getting anywhere.

I made several journeys over to Banbury to record my EP with Simon and Rob and stayed at Two Hoots B&B – the best B&B I have ever stayed in!

I remember my very first solo performance at Spring Harvest 2007 in the 8–11s venue with Andy and Catherine Kennedy. I was shaking like a leaf whilst I was performing but, at the same time, I'd never felt so comfortable on stage before. My EP was finally released in July 2007 and I decided to call it 'Made to be Me'. Those four words summed it all up for me. God had made me for such a time as this and I just wanted to be me . . . the real me. Not arrogant, not fake, just me . . . available and ready for God to use me in whatever way he wanted to.

I started doing gigs across the UK and I also worked part-time for Warrington Youth For Christ where I developed a self-esteem mentoring scheme for 14–16-year-old girls. I was being invited to speak at conferences and events all over the place, where all I could talk about was the way that God had transformed my life and how he could transform anyone's life if they wanted him to.

My third book, *The Something to Shout About Journal*, was then released, and by January 2008 I had finished writing and recording my debut album, *Have You Heard*? I did my first solo music video for one of my favourite songs on the album, 'Barbie Girl', and had filmed various other bonus features for the DVD that would accompany my album. My album was released in April 2008 and that's when things really started to roll.

Tim and I decided to move back to our home town of Warrington in November 2007. We both sensed that Warrington was the place for us to be. We moved to Stockport when we first got married because it was closer to where I was working when I was in tbc. But more than that, we wanted to have the time to establish ourselves as a married couple, away from familiarities and comfortable surroundings. When tbc came to an end, God began to strip some things away and we ended up realising there was nothing left for us in Stockport. That's when we sensed that God was telling us it was time to move on. We sold our house in Stockport and ended up renting and then living with Tim's parents whilst we waited for the house we were buying to be ready. We eventually (after a very long and complicated nine months of mayhem) moved into our new house in July 2008.

A part of us felt quite sceptical about moving back to Warrington. It was like we were taking a step back rather than taking a step forward. However, God spoke to me very clearly about it being a place where we were surrounded by close friends and family, so that during the busy times of our ministry we would always know we had a place to come home to, where we were loved and supported by the people closest to us. We have joined a great church (King's Church, Warrington) and are part of an amazing cell group, and Tim and I (oh . . . and our dog, Chester) have settled in and now call Warrington home.

So . . . I suppose you want to know what's next? We would quite like to know the answer to that question too! We know what God has called us to and we believe that the promises he has made to us will be fulfilled. All we know is that God has got a plan and a purpose for our lives and that he knows best. We're trusting him and allowing him to be in control. We are prepared to go wherever he sends us, and say whatever he tells us to say. We've learnt a lot of lessons over the years, both individually and together, and we're still learning. But more than ever we are excited about the future and can't wait to see what God has in store for us! Being in God's will is never an easy place to be. It's uncomfortable, it's risky, and sometimes it can be dangerous, but I'd rather be ready to make the most of opportunities than live with regret and wish I'd made more of it all.

In my bathroom I have some postcards with inspiring sayings written on them. Going to the toilet in our house has changed many people's lives and perceptions! I would like to give you the opportunity to read them for yourself:

'Live with intention.
Walk to the edge.
Listen hard.
Practice Wellness.
Play with abandon.
Laugh.
Choose with no regret.
Continue to learn.
Appreciate your friends.
Do what you love.
Live as if this is all there is.'
(by Mary Anne Radmacher)

This is the second one and I would challenge you to ask yourself this question every day:

'What would you attempt to do if you knew you could not fail?'
(*Unknown*)

" We have many organisers, but few agonisers;
Many players and payers, but few pray-ers;
Many singer, few clingers;
Lots of pastors, few wrestlers;
Many fears, few tears;
Much fashion, little passion;
Many interferers, few intercessors;
Many writers, few fighters.
Failing here we fail everywhere. "
[*Why Revival Tarries*' by Leonard Ravenhill]

Have I lived an ordinary life? Yes, I suppose I have. Did I have a good upbringing? Yes, I guess I did. Am I happy with my life? Yes, extremely happy. So, I hear you ask, why have I written this book?

I am an ordinary girl but I serve an extraordinary God and because of that and the way he is transforming me, I have the privilege of leading an extraordinary life. All the glory well and truly belongs to God.

ANOREXIA AND BULIMIA CARE

Anorexia and Bulimia Care (ABC) has been in existence in its present form since 1989. It is a national Christian organisation that provides help, advice and information for anyone who is suffering because of eating disorders: sufferers, their families, carers and professionals, regardless of faith.

ABC is able to offer help and support to sufferers and also has a dedicated help line (ACHE) for parents, guardians and anyone concerned about a child suffering with or showing signs of an eating disorder. They offer a professional, personal and caring service, from a team of staff with experience in eating disorders. They are also a resource for counsellors, support group leaders, church leaders, teachers, students and medical professionals.

Please, please, please, please, please . . . if you are struggling with any form of eating disorder, or you know someone who is struggling with an eating disorder, GET HELP NOW.

I was fortunate enough to have people around me who cared and got help before my problem got any worse. The first and hardest thing to do when you have a problem is to admit it to yourself. Only then can you begin to make a decision to do something about it. Don't wait a few months to see if it gets any worse . . . don't give yourself a second chance . . . act quickly and make the right choice. Recognise the signs and be honest with yourself.

Having a problem does not make you a failure – everyone makes mistakes at some stage or another. Don't be frightened of other people judging you; don't stay silent and just learn to live with it. The longer it goes on the worse it will get, so don't gamble with your life. I've been there, done that – believe me, it is not a pretty sight. Having an eating disorder doesn't make you more acceptable; it doesn't make you feel any better about yourself; it doesn't make you more beautiful. It may make you feel better for a short while but it doesn't last. I'm on my knees and begging you – take the high road, make the call and see the difference . . . please.

Help line: 01934 710679
Email: sufferersupport@anorexiabulimiacare.co.uk

ACHE help line: 01934 710645
Email: ache@anorexiabulimiacare.co.uk

Providence House
The Borough
Wedmore
Somerset
BS28 4EG

T: 01934 713789
E: help@anorexiabulimiacare.co.uk
W: www.anorexiabulimiacare.co.uk

1903222CD

9781860245565

9781860246210

9781844271405